Blood on the Forge

WILLIAM ATTAWAY

Blood on the Forge

Introduction by
Nicholas Lemann

ANCHOR BOOKS
DOUBLEDAY
New York   London   Toronto   Sydney   Auckland

An Anchor Book

PUBLISHED BY DOUBLEDAY

a division of Bantam Doubleday Dell Publishing Group, Inc.
666 Fifth Avenue, New York, New York 10103

ANCHOR BOOKS, DOUBLEDAY, and the portrayal of an anchor
are trademarks of Doubleday, a division of Bantam Doubleday Dell
Publishing Group, Inc.

Blood on the Forge was originally published by Doubleday, Doran &
Company in 1941. The Anchor Books edition is published by
arrangement with Doubleday & Company, Inc.

Anchor Books gratefully acknowledges the advice and guidance of
Charles R. Larson.

Library of Congress Cataloging-in-Publication Data

Attaway, William.
Blood on the forge/William Attaway
introduction by Nicholas Lemann
p.   cm.
1. Afro-Americans—History—Fiction.   I. Title.
PS3501.T59B55   1993
813'.52—dc20   92-31051
CIP

ISBN 0-385-42542-2
Text of *Blood on the Forge* Copyright 1941 by Doubleday,
Doran & Company
Introduction Copyright © 1993 by Nicholas Lemann
All Rights Reserved
Printed in the United States of America
First Anchor Books Edition: January 1993

1   3   5   7   9   10   8   6   4   2

For my sister Ruth

Introduction

By Nicholas Lemann

AFRICAN-AMERICAN CULTURE, which was essentially rural and Southern for centuries, has reinvented itself as urban and national. This reinvention has been a dramatic process, taking place all through the twentieth century, and it hasn't reached a true resting point yet. So it is nearly useless to attempt to understand black migration and urbanization as a completed story. About the best we can do with this enormous subject right now is to take it in slices; the experience of fully seeing and feeling one or two times and places along the way somehow casts an illumination across the whole vast history of it.

William Attaway's brutally powerful novel *Blood on the Forge* is rooted in specifics, in two ways: it takes place in settings that are limited to the point of claustrophobia, and intellectually it plainly belongs to a brief moment in the late Depression years. But all the issues it raises—issues of race relations, labor economics, and consciousness—seem absolutely pressing, perhaps all the more so because the particular circumstances Attaway described have vanished. *Blood on the Forge* is about the beginnings of a black unskilled, nonunion working class that no longer exists, and whose disappearance now appears to be one of the central tragedies of American life. So to read it today, half a century after its original publication, is to be nearly overwhelmed by what-ifs, might-have-beens, and never-weres.

The action of *Blood on the Forge* takes place during the first dramatic stage of the great black migration off the land. World War I had speeded up the pace of American industrialization while simultaneously calling to military duty a good part of the labor force, and the war caused immigration from abroad to be suspended. The resulting severe labor shortages in factories caused employers to turn their attention toward the Southern black belt as a source of strong-backed men. Labor agents—one of whom appears in *Blood on the Forge*—were dispatched to plantation country to recruit (this was a dangerous job, because their presence was unwelcome and in some states legally banned); black preachers were hired to sell their parishioners on the idea of migration; recruiting literature was circulated. Robert S. Abbott, the publisher of the *Chicago Defender*, a black paper that was widely circulated in the South, energetically promoted what he called "The Great Northern Drive," presenting migration as an almost biblical passage to true freedom.

In the South at the time, it was inconceivable that legal segregation would ever end. During the last years of the nineteenth century, blacks had effectively lost the right to vote through the institution of poll taxes and other qualifying tests. All public facilities were segregated. Blacks had no recourse to the legal system. They were barred from all but a handful of white-collar jobs. All social contact between the races had to take place in a context of black deference and servility, or white-on-black violence would immediately result. Millions of the worst-off, least-educated black Southerners were economically trapped in the notorious sharecropper system, under which they would work and live on land owned and supplies furnished by white planters, hoping to clear some money at the end-of-the-year "settle." Because of widespread cheating and, just after World War I, pestilences and world-wide price collapses, the usual result of the settle was that the sharecropper was even more deeply in debt to the planter, and more enmeshed in the system. It was common for Southern planters at the time to comment that the sharecropper system was even more economically advantageous to them than slavery had been.

One and a half million African-Americans moved from South to North during and just after World War I—about a fifth, in other words, of the final total for the great migration when it ended around 1970. Melody, Chinatown, and Big Mat Moss, the three half brothers who are the heroes of *Blood on the Forge*, migrate under especially dramatic circumstances: Big Mat kills a white "riding boss" who has insulted him, and they leave Kentucky for western Pennsylvania under cover of night, packed like cattle (or, as Attaway couldn't have known but we now can't help thinking, like concentration camp inmates) into a boxcar. But the general situation of the Moss brothers was fairly typical. There was no life for them in rural Kentucky other than the one they were living; opportunity and migration were practically synonymous. They were young and unencumbered enough to be mobile. Even so, it took a crisis—trouble with white folks—to get them to make the leap off the land.

Where blacks and whites live in proximity in the United States, there is usually racial tension, and this is especially true in places where the proximity is new. In the rural South in the early twentieth century, racial tension was a constant, nagging presence in daily life; lynchings, which were commonplace, were only the extreme manifestations of an ever-present nervousness about the nexus of race, sex, and violence. As soon as black migration to the Northern cities became significant, race relations arose as a big issue there too. In the North the tensions revolved around the competition for jobs and living space. There were riots in East St. Louis, Illinois, and Philadelphia in 1917, and in Chicago in 1919. *Blood on the Forge* chronicles the formation of that latter, Northern set of racial tensions.

While it's obviously a work whose sympathies are with the Left, *Blood on the Forge* is not "politically correct" by the lights of either its time or our own. When it was published, books about oppressed people were supposed to end hopefully, with the characters realizing that class struggle was the route to personal dignity and a brighter future. Aside from using a tiny bit of Marxist rhetoric to explain why the Moss brothers don't think this way, Attaway doesn't conform to the Left novelist's program at all: the brothers are shown to be on a trajectory of decreasing solidarity with their fellow workers, and they react to rising labor tension in the "wrong" way, that is, by either siding with capital or simply leaving the scene.

By today's standards, the characters in *Blood on the Forge* are perilously uncomplex: like John Steinbeck's heroes (and, to some extent, Richard Wright's Bigger Thomas), the Moss brothers have only a very few distinguishing personal traits—or, perhaps more accurately, fundamental drives. They are primarily understood as pawns on a great chessboard, individuals helplessly in the grip of vast, inexorable economic forces. Attaway makes a point of demonstrating that they don't fully grasp what's happening to them. And the thoughts and feelings that they do have seem, in part, fairly retrograde to present-day sensibilities: a need for love and work and dignity, yes, but also, in the case of the brothers, an aggressive, dominating, violent streak, and, for Attaway's female characters (nearly all of whom are prostitutes), a deep-seated dream of attaining the status of a respectable homemaker.

Such departures from strict literary-intellectual propriety do, however, vouch for Attaway's commitment to portraying the world of the migrants as he actually saw it, not as he thought it should be. Part of what's exhilarating about *Blood on the Forge* is that it is a product of an age when novelists took their literary training on the road, not in graduate school. Although William Attaway himself was a participant in the great black migration, having moved with his family at the age of five from Greenville, Mississippi, to Chicago, *Blood on the Forge* is in no sense his story: he was the son of a doctor and a schoolteacher, not a product of the sharecropper system. Obviously he made it his business to find out about a different part of the African-American experience before he wrote, because the settings of *Blood on the Forge* are portrayed with an almost unbearable vividness that could only be the product of firsthand observation.

The Moss brothers, as Attaway sees them, are, at their core, men of the land. Their meager lives in rural Kentucky are at least attuned to familiar, benevolent agrarian rhythms of harvest and husbandry. The giantlike Big Mat balances the satisfactions of work and marriage against the sorrows of childlessness and grief over his mother's death. Melody is a folk musician, Chinatown a mirthful soul. Their extended family situation—the three brothers apparently share a mother but have different fathers, and although two of them are unmarried and one married, they all live under the same roof—is presented as comfortable and unremarkable, in a way that calls to mind E. Franklin Frazier's uncensorious descriptions of the variegated living arrangements of black "peasants" in the rural South.

By contrast, everything about the industrial North seems unnatural and ominous for the brothers. Just as Frazier's tone shifted completely when he described black migrants' lives in what he called "the city of destruction," so too does Attaway's when Big Mat, Chinatown, and Melody arrive in a steel-mill town outside Pittsburgh. Now the landscape is one that has been profoundly violated by man: ugly, muddy, smoky, stripped, lit by an eerie furnace-glow. Wives and children are present in the town, but the emotional weight of Attaway's portrait is definitely not on the side of the family. All human relations seem to get caught up—and often ruined—in the cash nexus. The brothers' closeness is corrupted. Rather than sending for his wife back in Kentucky, Big Mat unhesitatingly takes up with a teenage prostitute. The transmogrification of male-female relations from love to a trade of cash for sex seems to be part of the capitalist territory: Attaway's unmistakable message is that the essential destiny of boys growing up in the town is the mills and of girls, the whorehouses.

A sense of foreboding pervades *Blood on the Forge* from the moment the brothers set out for the railroad junction and begin their middle passage to the North; and, indeed, their new home not only breaks their hearts and anesthetizes their minds (thanks to their constant self-administered doses of homemade corn liquor), it finally destroys them physically, one by one. First Melody loses the use of the hand that has always succored him by picking the strings of his guitar; then Chinatown's eponymous feature, his Asian-looking eyes, is extinguished; and finally Big Mat, who was distinguished by his sheer life-force, loses that. Attaway leaves no doubt but that Mat's death in a labor dispute is no less an industrial accident than were his brothers' manglings in the steel mills: all three were cannon fodder in the American industrial revolution.

In general, *Blood on the Forge* reminds us of how radically the New Deal and the Great Society—the one-two punch that created the American welfare state—transformed our society. Terms like Social Security, Medicaid, National Labor Relations Board, and Occupational Safety and Health Administration may sound dull and bureaucratic to the point of uselessness, but they did wipe out the world Attaway re-creates in *Blood on the Forge*, where people's bodies were simply used up and thrown away. No working people in this country have lives as horrible as those of Attaway's characters. But there is one realm in which the mill town in *Blood on the Forge* seems better than similar places in America today, and that is the realm of race relations.

The Moss brothers' Northern home is populated by a mix of Southern blacks, Mexican immigrants, and what we'd now call "white ethnics," all of whom are to some degree greenhorns, with a slight command of standard English and no real economic asset except

their physical strength. They share space in bunk-
houses; they work side by side in the mill (though
nearly all of the supervisory positions are reserved for
whites); interracial sex is common, at least in the
whorehouses; no one seems to remark on Mat's open
liaison with a Mexican girl. There is some amount of
interethnic banter and camaraderie, and the groups
seem to mix unself-consciously at the town's brutal
main social venue, fights to the death between trained
dogs. All of this would have been inconceivable in the
South at the time. In fact, it has never been typical of
life in the North, and still isn't today.

Granting that Attaway must be accurately portraying a racial situation that existed in at least some mill
towns, it's also obvious that he is operating at the level
of parable here. The races are driven apart in *Blood on
the Forge* by a specific force, labor unrest: most of the
whites join a union and go on strike, while Melody
and Chinatown stay home and Big Mat becomes a
strikebreaker, pathetically gratified by the opportunity to occupy a position of authority as a law-enforce-
ment official. All this causes the snake of racism to
enter the slag-garden of the town. At the end of the
book, as Melody and Chinatown get on another train,
headed for Pittsburgh, we can only imagine that their
new environment will be absolutely segregated—that
they'll live in an all-black neighborhood and work in a
for-colored-folks-only job, having left William Attaway's literary territory for August Wilson and John
Edgar Wideman's.

All over the urban North in the World War I era,

Southern blacks were used as strikebreakers, and were hated by unionized white labor. The message Attaway seems to have for us is that during the first part of the great migration, working-class whites started thinking of Southern blacks as niggers only after having perceived them as a threat to the unions or even to the ability to put food on the table. Economic competition preceded racial prejudice, in other words—though no doubt the whites didn't fully realize this, and believed what they were feeling was pure racial animosity. This was a Northern variation on an old Southern story: for a quarter century before the events of *Blood on the Forge*, the big economic and political interests of the South had fanned the flames of white racial prejudice as a way of circumventing economic populism. In *Blood on the Forge*, the distant, mysterious owners of the steel mill were doing the same thing.

The situations were slightly different in the South and the North, though. In the South, racism was the regnant political force in the mid-twentieth century and unions never really got started. In the industrial North, racism was not strong enough to short-circuit unionization but not weak enough to fade away, so the usual result was strong, segregated unions. When the next act of the great migration began, during World War II, when many more Southern blacks moved North than ever before, they were often greeted by a nearly absolute bar to employment in the skilled trades. Instead, they had to find unskilled jobs in factories that were often not unionized, or do domestic or custodial work. In addition, the greater the flow of migrants, the more strictly the Northern cities usually enforced residential segregation. The end result was big, crowded urban black ghettos filled with people whose support structures—family, work, education—were often very tenuous.

The unskilled industrial jobs in the Northern cities began to dry up in the late 1950s, and nearly disappeared entirely during the 1970s. People with good educations were often able to find their first white-collar jobs in government; many of the rest had no place to go. William Attaway's industrial hell of 1919 has been replaced by a hypersegregated, semi-abandoned, inner-city housing-project welfare hell, occupied, often, by the descendants of people like Melody, Chinatown, and Big Mat. This isn't an end result that Attaway predicted—*Blood on the Forge* is too close to the ground to engage in the making of predictions—but it certainly doesn't seem to represent a great shift in the course that Attaway say his particular strand of black history taking.

It's always tempting, when a bad moment in the past is re-created as vividly and powerfully as Attaway has re-created the one in *Blood on the Forge*, to wonder whether things might have turned out much better if only some crucial mistake hadn't been made. What if Melody, Chinatown, and Big Mat had joined the strike and wound up in a solid, integrated, unionized working class? What if this had been the typical experience of black migrants? Such questions are unanswerable, though, and it probably isn't much more than an interesting game even to ask them. History may be directable at the top level—Harry Truman could have decided not to drop the atomic bomb—but not below that; social history, involving millions of people's choices, usually moves with the inevitability of glaciers or tectonic plates. Throughout the great black migration, the idea of preventing it or reversing it was being discussed, by everyone from Southern planters to intellectuals to urbanologists to Northern politicians. Richard Nixon even obliquely mentioned it in a State of the Union address—a year or two after, unbeknownst to him, the migration had ended.

We can now recognize such talk as folly. Obviously, black America had to move off the land, and what disaster would have ensued if it hadn't can only be guessed at. In the same way, it won't do to react to the racial problems of the industrial North today by wishfully creating an interracial labor solidarity that never actually existed. As Attaway makes clear, the great black-white working-class coalition isn't something that almost coalesced; it was an impossibility, given the preceding racial history. The ways in which *Blood on the Forge* should inspire us are by reminding us that we have overcome what looked like insoluble social problems in the past, and by demonstrating that the time for us to address our difficulties is always now.

Blood on the Forge

One

He never had a craving in him that he couldn't slick away on his guitar. You have to be native to the red-clay hills of Kentucky to understand that. There the guitar players don't bother with any fingering; they do it by running a knife blade up and down the stops. Most of the good slickers down where he was born would say that a thin blade made the most music. But he liked the heft of a good, heavy hog sticker. It took a born player to handle one of those. And maybe that's why his mother changed his name to Melody when he got old enough for a name to mean something beside "Come get tit."

Nineteen-nineteen—early spring: the last time, there among the red-clay hills, he was to reach down his guitar. It was a hunger craving yanking at his vitals. That wasn't unusual; share-cropping and being hungry went together. He had never thought

about white pork, molasses and salt water corn-
bread as food anyhow. They were just something to
take the wrinkles out of his stomach. Maybe thinking like that had something to do with his not
growing up tall and hefty like his half brothers, Big
Mat and Chinatown—that and making music when
he should have been fighting over the little balls of
fat left in the kettle.

Chinatown was in the dust by the shack, playing mumblety-peg with the hog sticker. His back
was flattened against a tin patent-medicine sign
that covered the chinks in the cabin. Because the
tin held the heat of the last sun he rubbed his back
up and down and grinned. His gold tooth flashed.
There had never been anything wrong with his
teeth; he had just had a front one pulled to make
space for the gold.

Melody plopped down on the lopsided stoop
and arranged his guitar. Chinatown looked out of
the corners of his little slant eyes.

"What blues you chordin'?"

"Hungry blues." And Melody plucked the
thrown hog sticker out of the air.

"Won't be no more hungry blues come night."

Hattie came and stood in the doorway. She was
Big Mat's wife. The marks on her told that much.
But although she was hardly bigger than Melody's
music box nobody could take the spunk out of her.
She leaned against the doorjamb and rubbed one
bare foot against the other.

"I hear what you say, China."

"What you hear I say?"

"That you goin' out stealin' come night."

"You hear wrong, woman. I say ain't gonna be no more hungry blues, come night. An' you know why?"

" 'Cause we be doin' ninety days on the road gang for your thievin'?"

"Naw," squealed Chinatown, " 'cause, come night, we all be sleepin'." He laughed, and his gold tooth shone as he laughed, only you couldn't call it laughter by his face. His slant eyes and the tight skin drawing the lips back off his teeth made laughing his natural look.

"Maybe Mat bring somethin' back." Hattie sighed. "He gone over Moaningreen way to kill them ailin' hogs for Mr Johnston."

"Maybe he git a whole hog," said Chinatown. "They gonna die anyways."

"Mr Johnston ain't givin' niggers no well hog an' he ain't givin' 'em no sick hog. He ain't givin' 'em no hog a-tall." And with that Melody struck up a chord, running his knife the full length of the guitar. It was mellow, like the sound of hound dogs baying across a river.

> "*Done scratched at the hills,*
>   *But the 'taters refuse to grow. . . .*
> *Done scratched at the hills,*
>   *But the 'taters refuse to grow. . . .*
> *Mister Bossman, Mister Bossman,*
>   *Lemme mark in the book once mo'. . . .*"

There were more verses like that than any one man knew. And after each verse the refrain:

"Hungry blues done got me listenin' to my love one cry. . . .
Put some vittles in my belly, or yo' honey gonna lay down and die. . . ."

He quit singing to just slick a little while. There was no need to think; his hand wouldn't stop until it had found every minor chord in the box.

"It ain't no two ways about it," breathed Hattie. "Blues sure is a help."

"Hungry blues ain't nothin'," he told her, never stopping. "It ain't like you tryin' to blues away a love cravin' that git so mixed up with the music you can't know which is which."

"Lawd, now!" she breathed.

"Ain't never hear tell of a creeper singin' no love blues," said Chinatown through his golden grin.

"Ain't never seen no creeper without razor marks on him somewhere, you mean," said Hattie.

"There ain't no mark on me."

"Well, what you lay that to?"

"Reckon I jest too slick to git caught."

"You jest got more space to cook up devilment than anybody else. A body ought to be 'shamed to lay round in the dust all day, lettin' his two brothers go out in the fields and earn his somethin'-to-eat for him."

"I lazy, and they smart." He grinned. "I lazy

and hungry—they smart and hungry." He helped his point with a bigger grin.

Hattie did not know what to say. She fussed around with her feet. Then, snorting, she went into the shack. Chinatown winked at Melody.

From the southwest came a flock of coots, flying high, straining forward like all water fowl. All day they had been passing overhead, curving north. It would not be long before the wild ducks and geese would make the same passage. Chinatown looked up.

"When coots come afore the duck tomorrow goin' to bring bad luck." Extending his hands, he sighted along an imaginary rifle. "Bop! Bop! Bop!" He settled back, satisfied with the number of coots he had killed in his mind.

Hattie popped into the doorway. She had thought of the right answer for Chinatown. "It ain't needin' for none of us to be hungry, an' you with a hunk of gold in your mouth."

Chinatown looked scared, and Hattie watched him with satisfaction. She knew he would rather die than part with that shiny tooth but she was out to plague him.

"Maybe it ain't worth nothin'," he mumbled.

"It worth a full belly."

He could not look at her eyes. His toes searched the dust.

"I know what," she said.

"What?" mumbled Chinatown.

"Tonight I talk to Big Mat, so he yank it outen

your head and take it in to Madison."

Chinatown half rose. "No!" His voice went into falsetto and cracked. "I work in the bossman's fields all season for that tooth."

Hattie backed. "Onliest time you stir since is to look at that gold in the glass." She disappeared in the shack.

He sat back against the tin. After a time he mumbled, "Ain't no use in a man stirrin' round and gettin' all lathered up. He ain't gittin' no place."

He was talking to himself, but Hattie heard and called out, "Now what you tryin' to say?"

"Only seem like good sense to stay where you was in the first place and save yourself the trouble of comin' back."

She came to the door again. "How the crop goin' to git made?"

"We jest niggers, makin' the white man crop for him. Leave him make his own crop, then we don't end up owin' him money every season."

"Lawd, you never will be no good!" Hattie sighed. "Maybe you git straightened out if you gits a woman of your own to feed."

Melody entered the conversation in an old song:

> *"Now the berry always sweeter*
> *on the other man's bush. . . .*
> *What you reckon make that?"*

Chinatown guffawed. "Now that there the truth."

"Your poor dead maw musta had a conjure, to

set a bad egg like you without spoilin' the brook," she said.

"Better be careful not to say nothin' 'bout Maw when Big Mat around," Chinatown warned.

"Sure said he'd belt you," put in Melody.

"An' I ain't never knowed Mat to grin when he say somethin'," said Chinatown.

"Mat know he in the wrong," she scolded.

"Forgit about it," advised Melody.

"I got cause to talk as much as I please."

"Jest forgit about it."

"Mat jest afeared I goin' to talk about how come we ain't got no mule and what the reason we ain't got nothin' to cook up in the house."

To cut Hattie off Melody started up another spell of the blues. Maw hadn't been in the ground but about four weeks. Neither of them wanted to hear any talk about her or that mule. Talk brought back the homemade burial box, the light rain falling and the thud of falling clods still ringing in their ears as they went homeward across the pastures, before sunup Maw out pushing that one-mule plow, Chinatown sitting around in the dust, Melody dodging the fields for his guitar. They thought of it now. She had dropped dead between the gaping handles of the plow. The lines had been double looped under her arms, so she was dragged through the damp, rocky clay by a mule trained never to balk in the middle of a row. The mule dragged her in. The rocks in the red hills are sharp. She didn't look like their maw any more. Hattie went to work on the body with yellow hog-fat soap. Chinatown and Melody sat against the house and cried. Big Mat went away for a long time. He came back hog wild and he took a piece of flint rock and tore the life out of that mule, so that even the hide wasn't fit to sell.

Melody had fallen out on the ground and vomited and for three days afterward he couldn't hold food on his stomach. The sight of blood always acted on him like that.

Four weeks had stopped them from wailing. It was better for her to be in heaven, was Hattie's word on their maw, than making a crop for Mr Johnston. . . . Still, you couldn't stop her from working. If that mule went to the same place she did she probably started in right away to plow for God.

Mr Johnston said that they could not have any more food credit. He claimed their share of the crop for the next two years in payment for his mule. He didn't say where the crop was coming from when there was no animal to plow with. He didn't say how they were going to eat without food credit. All they could do was to wait for him to change his mind.

Hattie had kept at Big Mat, driving him crazy with her talk, blaming him for everything. One day it had taken both Chinatown and Melody to keep him from lighting into her with the butt end of a hoe. But he swore he'd belt her if she even mentioned Maw again.

Melody sang softer and softer. Soon he was just singing for himself. Going onto verse fifty, or thereabout, he got weary and barely hit the strings. He looked away over the rolling country to the place where the sun had about given up fighting the dark hills. Most of the country beyond Vagermound Common was bunched with crab-apple trees, posing crookedly, like tired old Negroes against the sky. Big Mat was going to come walking out of those hills, over the Vagermound Common, down the red, packed road that wound past their door. He was going to have a greasy sack over his shoulders, Melody hoped. To keep from hoping too hard about that sack he made out to play the wish game with Chinatown.

"China," he half sang, "you know where I wish I was at now?"

Chinatown hunched forward in the dust. He liked the wishing game. They had played at it all their lives, most times wishing they were at the grand places pictured in the old newspapers that livened the walls of the shack.

"Where at?" He grinned eagerly.

"Me—me," pondered Melody, "me—I wish I was in town. That's it—smack in town—and it's a Saturday noontime."

"What you be doin'?"

"Jest standin'—all made out in a white-checkered vest and a ice-cream suit, and you can't hardly see the vest for a gold watch chain. I got on shoes, too—yeller shoes with dimes in the toes. Man, man!"

"The gals is passing by. . . ." Chinatown tried to help.

"Naw, that ain't till evenin'. Now I aimin' to shoot some pool."

"You can't shoot no pool."

"But I wish I can," said Melody.

"Ain't you aimin' to make no music?"

"Jest aimin' to shoot some pool," he told him. "Course, I got my guitar with me, jest in case. But I'm feelin' too good to make my guitar cry."

"Now ain't that awful you can't make no music, and you feelin' good?" sympathized Chinatown.

"It don't make no never mind, 'cause my box is shinin' with silver, and the stops all covered with mother-of-pearl. An' everybody see me say that must be Mr Melody. They say howdy to Mr Dressin'-man Melody."

Hattie was in the doorway again.

"Stuff!" she snorted, but she was listening hard.

"What you do, come night?" asked Chinatown.

Melody thought hard and struck a long chord to make his thoughts swell with the music.

"Come night—come night . . . Well, I guess I spark around the gals and drink a little corn. Maybe I'm on a church picnic. The gal and me has got our bellies full and slipped away in the bushes at the edge of the river. Had the corn in my pocket all the time."

Chinatown had a pucker around his slant eyes.

"Goin' to drink anythin' but corn?" he asked hopefully.

Chinatown wanted him to put a bottle of red pop into the story. Chinatown lived on red pop whenever they were in Masonville. He had loved it from the first bottle given him by a white man who thought it would be funny to see a little slant-eyed pickaninny drink red pop. When asked how he liked it Chinatown had told the man:

"Taste kinda like your foots is 'sleep."

He was right.

"I say you goin' to drink anythin' but corn?" repeated Chinatown.

"Jest corn." Then, seeing how Chinatown was caught in the story, he added: "Maybe I mix it with a little red pop though."

"That make it good." Chinatown grinned.

It was deep dusk.

"Wish night gone and real night come on." Hattie sighed. "Guess I light the rag for Big Mat." Melody looked up, caught by the rhythm of her words. She went in to light the scrap in a dish of black tallow. The kerosene had been gone a long time.

Chinatown took an old quid out of his pocket. He wrapped it in a dried corn husk and tied the cigar-shaped mass with Johnson grass.

"Smoke always spoil my feelin' for eatin'," he said. He called to Hattie: "Hand me out a lighted stick."

"What you want a fire stick for?" she called back.

"Gonna set the house on fire." He laughed.

Grumbling, she brought a glowing twig.

"Ain't but one place you coulda got any to-bacco," she said. "You done found one of Mat's hunks o' chewin' tobacco and crumbled it up."

"That's right," he said.

"Mat take the hide off you."

"What for? He chewed this piece already about ten times."

"Well, can't say I hold no blame. . . . What I wouldn't give for a pinch of snuff under the lip!"

"Wish night gone and real night come on," Melody repeated. "That sound like the blues, Hattie."

"Too bad you didn't bring some wish snuff back with you from Wish Town," was her answer.

"Night creep up like a old woman," Melody said softly to himself. "Can't see her—can't hear her. She jest creep up when your back turned."

"Smoke makin' me light in the head. My stomach growlin'. Guess that mean I got fast business in some white man's smokehouse." Chinatown snuffed his smoke. He got to his feet, cleaning his hands by spitting on them and wiping them on his overalls.

"She got on a black skirt," Melody dreamed. "She black, too, so's you can't see her legs when she shackle her skirt to the floors o' the earth."

"Keep the kettle bilin', Hattie," said Chinatown. "Bilin' water for meat or for buckshots."

Melody began to sway.

"At night the hills ain't red no more. There ain't no crab-apple trees squat in the hills, no more land

to hoe in the red-hot sun—white the same as black.
. . . Where the mule gone at? He only a voice in
the pasture land. . . ."

Of a sudden he became conscious of what he was
doing. He grabbed for the guitar. "Listen, China;
listen, Hattie—listen what I'm doin'." He went on
lightly: "Now the chigger ain't nothin' but bite. All
the crickets is is a big chirp in the grass. Night bird
call out the deathwatch. . . . Night-flyers is glow
buckles on the garters of old creepin' night. The
mosquitoes is her swamp-fever sting. . . . But it
don't last long, 'cause she say, 'Git along,' an' be
nothin', 'cause black ain't nothin', an' I is
black. . . ."

"Hallo, hallo . . ." It came like an echo lost in
the hills beyond Vagermound.

Hattie was peering into the night, listening.

"Hallo, hallo . . ." the echo answered itself.

"It's Big Mat," she cried.

"Well, git the kettle bilin', woman," cried
Chinatown. "He ain't holler lessen he got somethin' in a sack."

> "*Nigger, nigger never die.*
> *Black face and shiny eye,*
> *Kinky hair and pigeon toe—*
> *That the way the nigger go. . . .*"

Because he was blacker than his half brothers the
white share croppers' kids had sung that little chant

at him. They had said that Big Mat's father must have been a lump of charcoal. And Big Mat had learned to draw to a safe distance within himself everything that could be hurt. The years had given him a shell. But within that tight *casure* his emotions were under great pressure. Sometimes they broke through, and he filled with red madness—like a boar at mating—hog wild. Few folks had seen him like that. To almost everybody but his close kin he was a stupid, unfeeling giant, a good man to butcher hogs and veal cattle. Melody alone knew him completely. Melody, from his dream world, could read the wounds in Big Mat's eyes.

Now seven carcasses glistened on the sacks at Big Mat's feet. Flies struggled in the sticky blood that oozed from the box of entrails. He threw the chain around the hind leg of the last hog. Passing the free end of the chain over the low branch of a tree, he began to hoist the struggling, squealing animal off the ground. Out of the corners of his eyes he saw Mr Johnston and the riding boss. Mr Johnston had always been a landowner, but the riding boss had been a poor white share cropper. Big Mat remembered him as a little ragged boy singing the hated chant. The two men stood in the shade of the barn, mixing their talk and spit. That talk was about him. He could see it in their little gestures. So he bent closer to the chain, lifting the hog in easy jerks. When the hog was well off the ground Mat fastened the chain to a stake and reached down into the box of guts for his knife.

"Oh, Mat," called Mr Johnston.

"Yessuh?" Mat waited.

Mr Johnston came toward him.

"This here's the last hog, ain't it?"

"This the brood sow, suh."

"Well, I want to catch her blood."

Mat went and got a bucket and set it under the hanging animal.

"Figger to make some blood sausages," said Mr Johnston. "Damn good eatin' when they made right."

Mr Johnston stood watching while Big Mat wiped the knife across the hog's teats. The animal had grown quiet. Its little eyes sucked back out of sight. The snout dripped a rope of saliva halfway to the ground. Big Mat touched the hog's neck tentatively with the point of the knife. The animal quivered. The shining rope broke and made a bubble on the ground.

"Mr Johnston."

"What it is, Mat?"

"This here the last hog, and the sun almost down. I was jest wonderin'——"

"Say what's on your mind, boy," said Mr Johnston.

"My folks is waitin'——"

"For what?"

"For me, Mr Johnston. They hungry. . . ."

"Go on."

"If I could jest scald this one and leave the

butcherin' until tomorrow—take somethin' home to my folks . . ."

Mr Johnston spat his quid into the box of entrails.

"Well, that there's a good idee, Mat. What you figger on takin' home?"

"Why, anythin' you gives me, suh." Mat played the knife over the sow's throat. The animal held its breath and then gagged. Saliva ran like unraveling silk.

"What makes you think I'm goin' to give you anythin', Mat?"

Big Mat did not answer.

Mr Johnston said, "It ain't my fault your folks ain't got nothin' to eat."

The knife point found a spot on the hog's neck.

"I figger this here labor can jest go on what you owe me for my mule."

The blade slid out of sight. The haft socked against the bristled neck. A quick wiggle of the knife found the great blood vessel. Big Mat drew the blade. Dark blood gushed in its wake. Mr Johnston looked admiringly.

"You know the needs of a knife, Mat," he said.

Big Mat stood watching the hog bleed. He shifted the bucket a trifle with his toe.

"Mr Johnston."

"Yes, Mat?"

"How we goin' to make a crop this year? We already late on plowin'."

Mr Johnston grinned. "Well, Mat, I figger on

you all makin' a good crop with corn and molasses cane."

"We got to have a mule, suh."

Mr Johnston's eyes grew small and sharp. "Looka here, I contract with you for a crop. It ain't my business how you make it. Them hills has always growed a crop and they 'll grow one this season if you folks have to scratch it outen the bare rocks."

So Big Mat told him what he already knew about the land: "It ain't jest the mule, suh. It's everythin'. Wind and rain comin' outen the heavens ever' season, takin' the good dirt down to the bottoms. Last season over the big hill the plow don't go six inches in the dirt afore it strike hard rock. Stuff jest don't come up like it use to. Us 'll have a hard time makin' it on our share, mule or no—a hard time. . . ."

Mr Johnston caught Big Mat with his eyes. He came forward. Big Mat looked doggedly into the hard eyes. For a long second they hung on the edge of violence.

Mr Johnston said, "You ain't kickin', are you, Mat?"

Big Mat's eyes dropped to the bloody entrails. He presented a dull, stupid exterior.

"Nosuh, I ain't kickin'."

Mr Johnston smiled and drew out a plug. He bit a chaw and settled it in his cheek to soften.

"Mat," he said, "you know I don't have nothin' but niggers work my land. You know why?"

"Nosuh."

"Well, they's three reasons: niggers ain't bothered with the itch; they knows how to make it the best way they kin and they don't kick none."

The hog suddenly started its final death struggles. It threshed about on the chain, throwing blood in a wide circle. Mr Johnston jumped back. Big Mat grabbed hold of the animal's ears and held the big body steady.

"They don't jump till they 'most dead," said Big Mat.

Mr Johnston laughed. "What I say jest past your understandin', Mat—slips off your head like water offen a duck's back."

"Yessuh."

"You a good boy though. What I really come over here for is to tell you I'm goin' to let you have a mule tomorrow."

"Yessuh." Big Mat's outward self did not change, but his heart jumped. A mule was life.

"An' about what's on the book against you—you send them brothers of yourn over here. They can work some of it off. Give them fifty cents a week to boot. That 'll keep you goin'."

"Yessuh."

"You kin take along a bag of them guts when you go. Throw the rest of them back to the other hogs."

Mr Johnston started toward the house. He turned. "Oh, Mat, my ridin' boss tells me there some jacklegs around, lyin' to the niggers about how much work they is up North. Jest you remember how I treat you and don't be took in by no lies."

It was dark when Big Mat picked up his greasy sack and started for home. The moon would not be up yet, but he knew the rolling hills by night. His feet would find the road. Deep inside him was his familiar hatred of the white boss, but the thought of a mule was hot, like elderberry wine. Against the dark sky the darker crab-apple trees kept pace with him as he walked. When he reached the edge of Vagermound Common he threw back his head and gave a long "Hallo . . . hallo . . ."

"We seen you comin' way yonder," said Chinatown. "The pig taller was shinin' green all over your face."

Big Mat grunted and lowered the sack six and a half feet to the floor. There was a *squoosh* and smell that made Chinatown's mouth water.

"Chitterlin's! Man and sweet Jesus!" cried Chinatown. He scraped a handful of the white fat off of the outside of the sack, cramming the white stuff into his mouth.

Hattie hefted the load.

"How many of them ailin' hogs was it?"

"Eight and a brood sow," grunted Big Mat.

"Eight and a brood sow, and all you git is a little sack o' entrails!" she exploded. "Not nary a head?"

"Claim I owe him the labor."

"What for he claim that?"

"Labor go ag'inst what he got us on the books for."

"One sack of chitterlin's better 'n none at all." Chinatown grinned. "Git them cleaned and biled afore we talk about the rest."

"What he do with the other eight entrails?" asked Hattie.

"Git on, woman, afore I eats raw hog guts," said Chinatown. He grabbed up the sack and emptied it into a bucket.

"What he do with the rest?" insisted Hattie.

"Do it matter?" Melody told her.

"He goin' to feed the other guts to the well hogs," said Big Mat.

Chinatown laughed and clucked his gold tooth.

"He can't git nowhere, feedin' his hogs to his hogs."

"Jest the guts," droned Mat.

Chinatown laughed again.

They all helped to prepare the chitterlings for the pot, splitting some of them down the middle, turning others inside out, squeezing the still-warm mess onto the sack. Then some of the fat had to be scraped off. Hattie scolded as she scraped.

"You should of seen Mr Johnston's wife. She ain't so much of a chigger like him. She give you a hog head and some black-eyed peas to go 'long with it even."

"Keep shut, Hattie," said Melody. "He got more

sense than to talk to a white lady—don't care who she is."

"It's dangerous," agreed Chinatown. " 'Member young Charley from over in the next county got lynched jest 'cause he stumble into one in the broad daylight. She scream."

"I stumble anywhere I feels like it," declared Hattie.

"You is a colored woman. White man ain't gonna do much to a colored woman in daylight. He gonna do somethin' to her at night," said Chinatown.

"I kills anybody I catch creepin' round my back door," grunted Big Mat.

"Glad I got a he-man," sang Hattie.

"Anybody I catches creepin'," repeated Mat.

"I sure got me a man," chanted Hattie.

"Melody and me was in town after the big rains last," said Chinatown, "when who come walkin' along but old Mrs Johnston. The plank walk so narrow we have to jump out in the mud to keep from brushin' her."

"Huh!" grunted Big Mat.

"Wasn't no use in takin' a chance," said Melody.

"Huh!" he grunted.

"My man," chanted Hattie.

"Maybe he'd of grabbed her by the arm." Chinatown laughed. "Maybe he'd of grabbed her by the arm and say, 'Goin' my way, Mrs Johnston? I'm Big Mat, who make crop for your husband.' "

"China, you reckon any lady who sleep with a polecat like Mr Johnston is white underneath her clothes?"

"Can't say. Ain't never looked underneath her clothes." He laughed.

Big Mat looked from behind heavy brows.

"Shut that filthy talk," he growled.

Chinatown winked at Melody.

"He and Mr Johnston is pals now."

"He goin' to let us have another mule," announced Big Mat.

"Lawd today!" gasped Hattie.

A quick glance passed between the men. No words were big enough to give their thoughts meaning.

"He goin' to work China and Melody half a day in his own fields to lessen what on the book against us—give 'em fifty cents a week to boot."

Here was something small enough for talk.

"Good news! Good news! What you hold it so long for?" demanded Hattie.

"Kin git me a sack o' tobacco," Melody dreamed.

Hattie's eyes were far away. "I won't know how to feel with a little pinch under the lip all the time agin," she said.

"We kin have hog meat in the house on Sunday," cried Melody.

"An' me thinkin' this was the last eatin' we was gonna do for a long time," said Hattie.

"Wait awhile," said Chinatown. "What for he so good to us all of a sudden?"

"What you want to know all that for?" asked Hattie. "You afeared of workin' in the fields?"

"It ain't natural for a white man to git mealy-mouth overnight."

"Don't look the gift hoss in the mouth," cried Hattie.

"I'm pass the mouth now. I'm lookin' right down his throat."

"You try to git funny 'bout ever'thin'," she told him.

Melody's forehead wrinkled.

"It do look queer, him bein' so hard on us and then gittin' soft all of a sudden."

Hattie smacked him across the face with a piece of hog gut.

"Now you all got me to wonderin'," she cried. "Whyn't you jest keep shut and leave me git happy for once?"

"What he say?" said Melody to his brother. "Tell us ever'thin' he say."

"Yeah, what he say?" seconded Chinatown.

"Ain't say nothin' much."

"Musta said somethin'," said Melody.

"Ain't he say why he git easy on us?" asked Chinatown.

"Ain't say nothin' much."

"Sure is funny." Chinatown laughed.

"What's funny?" said Hattie.

"Mr Johnston run poor white trash off his land for nothin'. His ridin' boss carry a whip to hit folks for nothin' and throw them off the land when they too old to make good crop. Now he got a good reason to git mad and he ain't."

"Maybe he got religion," said Hattie.

Big Mat was scraping hard on the chitterlings.

"Come to think," he said, "there was somethin' else——"

"About you owin' him the labor?" said Hattie.

"Naw, he say that for us not to listen to any jackleg that come around. Say there some jacklegs tryin' to git niggers to go up North and work."

They all grinned.

With so many working, it wasn't long before the chitterlings were boiling in the black iron kettle. Then there was nothing more to do but wait and watch the kettle sway on its hook in the fireplace.

Hattie snuffed the lighted rag in the dish.

"No use burnin' taller, with a cob fire agoin'." She pulled up a homemade barrel chair and sat watching the kettle.

Chinatown dragged the pallet from the corner where he and Melody slept. There was a white iron bed, but it was for Big Mat and Hattie.

"When they be done?" asked Chinatown.

"Come mornin', they be done," said Hattie.

He lay on the pallet, with his head not far from the steaming kettle.

"Don't want to miss none of the smell, case I drop off," he explained.

"Sleep, boy. I wake you," promised Hattie.

Sitting on the floor, his back against the side of the warm chimney, Melody listened to the night noises through the open door. His eyelids drooped halfway and stayed like that.

"Hand my Bible, woman," grunted Big Mat.

Big Mat was a big bag of muck dumped on a chair. His face was an old piece of harness leather left a whole season to blacken and curl in the sun and rain.

"I say hand my Bible," he repeated.

So Hattie handed him the backless Bible, and he was mumbling to himself, as if he didn't know the whole thing by heart.

"You kin see all right?" she asked.

"Huh."

"You ain't bad off, are you, Mat?"

"Why you ask?"

"You studied your Bible this mornin'."

"Watch the pot," he grunted.

"You ought to feel good, Mat—us gittin' a mule agin."

"Huh."

"Lawd, it's come down on you agin!" She sighed.

"What come down on me?"

"You feelin' the curse on you—I kin tell."

"The curse always on me."

Melody listened. He couldn't tell Big Mat differently. He didn't know what made Big Mat go childless year after year. Six springs Hattie was big but she dropped her babies before they got together enough to be human. To another man that wouldn't have meant what it did to Big Mat. Mat studied the good book. He figured he knew when the Lord was picking on a man. Melody didn't know differently. For some reason his mind snapped back to a day in the fields—a day long gone.

A light spring rain fell before the sun. It was soon gone. The mist was rolling up from the new-turned furrows when Big Mat led the way to the fields. Melody shifted the mule harness from one shoulder to the other, and they walked through the hard dirt. The mule saw them a long way off and laughed like mules laugh when they have been lonely.

He hitched up the mule while Mat was getting an old quid loose from his pocket. It was almost white from chewing. Mat stood there, rolling it around in his jaws to get it so it would chew without powdering up. He saw the plow was ready.

"Whyn't you go help Maw in the back-door garden?"

"Two do more work out here."

"She gittin' old. Set the turnips for her."

Melody didn't leave right away. He went with Big Mat to the one good strip of the farm, heavy muck land next to the bottoms. He walked behind him on the first row, breaking the cool clods with his bare feet. At the turn Mat stopped to shift his chew and spit a long, juicy stream. They stood ankle-deep in the broken muck and sniffed the air that blew in from the bottoms. Right then Melody was feeling the earth like a good thing in his heart.

"Make you forgit you just a nigger, workin' the white man's ground," he said.

"This little strip of ground grow anythin'," said Mat.

Melody picked up a clod and tasted it.

" 'Member how we used to eat dirt when we was little scapers? It still taste good."

"Muck ground git big every year jest like a woman oughta."

"Mat, I got a big feelin' like the ground don't belong to the white boss—not to nobody."

"Maybe muck ground my woman."

Melody began to feel sad but he didn't want his guitar to do anything about it. Every once in a while he would get filled up like this with a feeling that was too big to turn into any kind of music.

"You know, Mat—wish I'd 'a' had a chance to sit at a schoolhouse like white kids—all the year round."

"Muck ground jest a woman."

"Man had oughta know book learnin'——"

"Only muck ground never fail if you plows it——"

". . . so's he kin know how to say what he's feelin'."

"Git big if you plows it."

"Guess I oughta been white."

"Jest as well I was born a nigger. Got more misery than a white man could stand."

Melody had to look at him.

His voice was so deep it was like a slow roll on a drum.

Melody came back from that long-gone day, and Hattie was talking. . . .

"Mat . . ."

"Huh?"

"Maybe it's gonna be different. I—I feels funny—like every time it's gonna happen."

"It ain't never happened so late."

"I ought to know—six times—I ought to know."

"How you know?"

"Six times I feels funny. Now I feels funny."

"Keep shut, woman." He was looking around, as though there were a stranger to hear. Hattie's eyes rolled in her head as she followed his fearful glances. The Bible shut with a snap. She jumped. He said, half ashamed, "Damn a woman who can't even keep the pot astirrin'."

"Mat . . ."

"Huh?"

"You reckon six is enough for the curse?"

"I don't reckon nothin'. The Lawd don't love no child of sin. That's why he don't love me. That's why he put the curse on me."

"You reckon the curse on Melody and China-town too. They wasn't studded right."

"The Lawd jest pick on the first born."

"Why that?"

"That always the way. The curse on me for them too. I try to be a good man—but he don't care nothin' 'bout that."

"Lawd, Lawd, the curse on us for always?"

"I got to preach the gospel—that the only way."

"Mat, maybe if you preaches on Sundays from now on—maybe this time ever'thin' be all right."

"I can't preach to nobody."

"But you studies the Bible."

"I can't preach, no matter how much it's inside me."

"But, Mat, you kin try—jest so's ever'thin' be all right jest this one time."

"I can't."

"Mat——"

"If I trys to preach 'fore folks it all jest hits against the stopper in my throat and build up and build up till I fit to bust with wild words that ain't comin' out."

The firelight was doing crazy things to his face.

"Mat——"

"Keep shut!"

He struck her across the mouth with the back of his hand. The blow didn't make any noise. Hattie didn't make any noise.

"Damn . . . damn . . ." he was muttering. He went out through the open door. "Damn a woman who can't even keep a pot astirrin'," he groaned, half ashamed, in the night.

Melody went to sleep.

Hattie's voice woke him a second later, but hours had passed. The gray was in the doorway. China-town was stirring.

"Up now, you lazy scapers. They's done!"

The air was steamy with a hot-manure smell, done-chitterling smell.

The sun was coming up. Nine white carcasses gleamed, gaping open, split down the middle, head and feet gone. They were like nine small human bodies. Big Mat worked as fast as he could. There were hams to be sugar-cured, sides of white fat meat to be brined in kegs, shoulders to be kept fresh in a hillside cave, ends to be pickled, scraps to be thrown in the hog slops. He cut the meat and stacked it neatly.

The sun was overhead when he wiped the knives and cleavers and got to his feet. The work was finished. This was the day Mr Johnston was going to give him a mule. In his pocket was a length of raw-hide. He would use it to lead the animal home. If he hurried there would be time to break a little ground before dark. He thought of the little strip of muck next to the bottoms. He would walk behind the plow. The soil would be damp. It was a good thing to break the ground for seeding and watch the land get big. Field, animal or man—the seed should be sunk in the spring for a good crop. Maybe this time Hattie would not drop his child dead. Seven was a lucky number.

When he came to the back door of the big house he took off his hat to twist in his hands. Mrs Johnston came to the back-door screen. Mr Johnston was in town, she told him—had left before daybreak. No, she didn't know anything about a mule. But the riding boss would know. He was somewhere in the fields. She hurried back to her kitchen duties.

He stood awhile, then he followed the split-rail fence where it wound over the hills.

Big Mat sat on the split-rail fence and looked at the three mules. They stood together, so they could fan the flies from one another's faces. Two were young and fat. They would make a fine team. The third was old and rawboned. That would be the one Mr Johnston meant to give him. Still, that old mule would outwork a horse twice his weight. For a long time Big Mat sat trying to imagine himself owning the brace of young mules, working every acre of the farm, combing down their coats until they were smooth as smooth. He would hitch them to a two-wheel wagon and drive Hattie to church every Sunday. Chinatown and Melody could sit astride those mules and make every church picnic in the county. His face did not change with those thoughts, but his eyes were alive.

A sweat bee buzzed over the mules' backs. They started a nervous kicking.

"Git away from my two mules," said his mind.

He climbed down the fence. Snatching off his hat, he struck at the sweat bee. The mules kicked up their heels and ran to the middle of the field.

"What the hell you doin' to them mules, boy?"

It was the riding boss. Galloping up to the fence, he held a short quirt ready in his hand.

"It was a sweat bee," said Big Mat.

"Be damned to that!" said the riding boss. "Git on back to your work."

"Work all done."

"Well, git on home."

"Mr Johnston said I could have a mule."

The riding boss turned red in the face. His neck swelled. Stiff legged, he dismounted. He walked up to Big Mat.

"Maybe you don't know who you talkin' to, boy—givin' me short talk."

Big Mat did not answer.

"Say, 'suh,' "ordered the riding boss.

"Yessuh."

The riding boss started to turn away.

"Got to keep steppin' on you niggers, or you git outa hand—forgit jest who you talkin' to."

"Nosuh, I ain't forgot," said Big Mat. "Us used

to play together when your folks was share-croppin' next to mine."

The riding boss turned and slashed the quirt across Big Mat's face. He felt like he had struck unfeeling, dead flesh.

"Damn fool!" he muttered. "Don't even know enough to back offen a whip."

Big Mat looked out of dull eyes, watching the quirt from a great distance within himself. A picture of the unplowed land came into his mind. When the land was not being worked folks were hungry. Maybe after this trouble Mr Johnston would take back all he had promised. Hattie and the boys should not have to go hungry when they were not to fault. He wondered why he had talked up to the riding boss. He had known what would happen.

"Well, what you waitin' for? Git!" snapped the riding boss.

"I'm sorry for what I done," muttered Big Mat. "If I could wait around for my mule I could git in some plowin' 'fore dark."

"If Mr Johnston got good sense you won't never git another mule," said the riding boss. "You'd be run off the land if I had my say. Killin' a animal worth forty dollars, 'cause a nigger woman got dragged over the rocks——"

The riding boss fell to the ground, blood streaming from his smashed face. He struggled to get to his feet. A heavy foot caught him in the side of his neck. His head hung over his shoulder at an odd

angle. The quirt remained in his hand, standing upright. Then the hand opened, and the quirt fell out
on the ground.

Big Mat stood over the unconscious man, eyes
almost crossed by inner disturbance. Then the
red mist fell away from his vision. He saw the riding boss. For a minute he did not connect the fallen
man with himself. Then he knew what he had
done. "A dead one," was his first frightened
thought. Then he saw the uneven movement of
the red throat, the fluttering blood bubbles at the
nose. The riding boss would live to lead the lynch
mob against him. That thought shot through him,
shaking him loose. In a panic he started to lope
across the meadow. His feet, like his mind, led him
aimlessly in a crisscross pattern. One of the mules
began to cry. The sound echoed in a grove of wil-
lows far off in the hills. Big Mat stopped. He looked
at the mules. They stared. He ran back and tied
the length of rawhide around the old mule's lower
jaw. Then he was leading the animal away to the
hills. There was no good reason for it. But this was
the day he was supposed to get a mule.

Big Mat knew the red hills as though they were
his own back yard. But this day every place was
strange. He was hunted.

Pushing his great muscles beyond their power,
he yanked the mule over the hills. Every crooked
crab-apple branch seemed to menace, sending him
onward. But his aimlessness could not throw him
out of an inner groove. He moved within a great

circle. And when evening came he found himself at no great distance from his farm.

A great calm settled on him.

Noise carries a long way in the hills. Chinatown and Melody raised their heads to listen. Stuffed with chitterlings, they had been dozing in the sun, waiting for Big Mat to come back with the mule. It wasn't Mat, they decided; this noise was the shuffle-clop of an old horse trotting way in the rear of the sound he was making. Like dry-land turtles, they waited, with their heads off the ground, to see who would come jogging along the road.

"Can't be anybody avisitin'," Melody said.

The shuffle-clop was just around the far elbow of the road. They got set to wave.

"Headed for town," remarked Chinatown.

A stranger, a white man in a flapping black hat, astride a black nag. They stopped their hands in mid-air.

"Well, look yonder!" breathed Chinatown.

Strangers never passed by their house; they were too far back in the hills.

The stranger saw them in the dust and raised his reins. They got to their feet. Chinatown took off his old hat and knucked at his forehead. The stranger rode near. Chinatown began to grin. He wasn't tickled. He always bent his back and grinned a little for white folks.

"Hallo, boys."

"Howdy, suh."

"Howdy, Cap'n."

Hattie was in the doorway.

"Afternoon, ma'am," said the stranger.

Hattie looked scared.

Chinatown looked out of the corners of his eyes. Melody was already on guard. The man had not called her "A'nty," as white folks did when they didn't know her first name. What kind of trick was this man up to?

"What we kin do for you, Cap'n?" asked Chinatown.

"You the Moss boys, ain't you?" said the man.

"We the Moss boys, Cap'n."

"I was told there was three of you."

"They's three of us, Cap'n—only one ain't here."

"Which one of you is called Big Mat?"

"He the one ain't here, Cap'n."

"He's the head of this family, I was told."

"That's right, Cap'n."

"Then he's the one I wanted to see."

Hattie spoke from the doorway.

"We ain't seen hide or hair of Big Mat for a long, long spell, suh."

"That there the truth," spoke up Chinatown. "He a good-for-nothing—always run off when it come time to make up the ground for crop."

The man smiled. "It's all right. Black George, down the way, told me to see you boys."

"Black George . . . Black George . . ." pondered Chinatown.

"Said he was a friend of yours."

Chinatown turned to Melody.

"You ever hear of anybody down the way name Black George?" he asked.

"Cain't say as I have."

The white man turned to Melody.

"Look here," he said, "I ain't got all day. You think you can deliver a straight story?"

"Reckon I kin, suh."

"Can you keep your mouth shut too?"

"Reckon so, suh."

The man gave a broad look around the yard.

"I'm from up North," he said.

Chinatown and Melody stared. This was the first real jackleg they had ever seen.

"They need men up there—good men—all they can get. If Big Mat speaks for this family tell him they can use him and all the other able menfolks in his house."

"If I see him I tell him," said Melody.

"Dammit!" cried the man, "you don't have to be cagey with me. I'm your friend."

"Sure, Cap'n." Chinatown grinned.

"Look here, are you boys satisfied with the way you're getting on around here?"

"Oh, yessuh, we satisfied," cried Chinatown warily.

"Yessuh, they ain't kickin' none," came Hattie's warning voice from the doorway.

"How much crop you make last year?" asked the man.

"Put in nigh thirty acres," Melody told him.

"That's good," said the man. "Must have made yourself a couple hundred dollars or so."

"Reckon that's right, but Mr Johnston keeps the book. He don't let us see what's writ in it."

"Well, don't you know how much he gave you?"

"Nosuh, he say what we made, and what's writ against us leaves us owin' him."

"It don't make any difference," said the man. "Just suppose you made two hundred dollars. Up North in the mills you three would make more 'n that much in a month."

Chinatown grinned his disbelief. Hattie gave a little snort and went into the house.

"You boys want to make that kind of money, don't you?"

"Sure do, Cap'n." And Chinatown grinned behind his hand.

The man reached back in his pocket and pulled out a roll of bills. It was more money than Chinatown had ever thought was in the world. The permanent grin almost left his face as the man shucked off a ten-dollar bill and gave it to him.

"Now you think I'm on the level?"

"Yessuh—yessuh, Cap'n," stuttered Chinatown.

"The freight train will stop at Masonville Junction at midnight. That's tonight. That's where you boys board her for the North."

"But there be trouble if we tries to leave," said Melody.

"Won't nobody see you if you look spry," said the man. "Then you're in a sealed boxcar that won't be opened until you're out of the state."

"Maybe Big Mat won't come," Melody told him.

"He'll come if you tell him the thing straight, like I told you."

"What about Hattie?" Melody asked. "That's his wife."

"He can send for her later. Can't transport no women."

"Yessuh."

The man climbed back onto his horse.

"Now don't forget—tonight—Masonville Junction. I'll be there to put you on board."

A white man in a flapping black hat, astride a black nag—he was gone. They stood looking after him full twenty minutes after the hills had muffled the sound of the black nag's hoofs. Then Chinatown gave a whoop and waved the ten-dollar bill high in the air.

"Lawd! And I thought only niggers was dumb."

Hattie came flying to the doorway.

"What the fuss?"

"That jackleg give us this here for foolin' him."

"Lawd-a-mercy!" cried Hattie. "Lemme git a tin can and bury that money back in the hills."

"I'm keepin' this in my pocket, woman," cried China.

"Fool! He come back for it sure," said Hattie.

"Let him come back," said China. "When I hear him comin' I'm off to the hills."

Chinatown danced around until he wore himself out. Then he dropped, puffing and blowing, to the ground.

"Must be a lot of that kind of up-North money," said Melody.

"Glad some of it stray off down this way." Chinatown grinned.

"You reckon that white man tellin' the facts?"

"Don't know."

"Maybe we ought to be at Masonville Junction tonight."

"You talkin' crazy," cried Hattie. "Big Mat ain't just going to pick up and walk off the land."

"There a snake under the door sill somewhere," said Chinatown. "Man have to kill himself workin' to make the kind of money he was talkin' about."

"But if he was speakin' facts," said Melody, "us makin' a year crop money in one month——"

"Well, supposin' so . . ."

"Think what we have in a season."

"Supposin' so . . ."

"We have all the money in a year."

"Supposin' so . . ."

"In two years we got enough to fill a corn crib."

"Supposin' so . . ."

Melody got heated up.

"What you mean by that 'Supposin' so'? Why, China, in two years you wouldn't have to do no work."

"I don't do no work now." He laughed. Then he rolled like a pony in the dust, tickled over how he had tricked Melody.

"When Big Mat come we go into town and buy up some stuff," said Hattie.

"Gonna drink red pop till I falls out," sang Chinatown.

"A big can of snuff," said Hattie.

"Red pop, fried fish, a big box of candy all tied up in red ribbon."

"Maybe I git some calico," said Hattie, looking down at her torn gray dress.

"Hold on, woman!" cried Chinatown. "This money ain't for wastin'."

"What you hanker for most, Melody?" asked Hattie.

"Reckon I wants a new E string for my box," he told her.

Away off in the hills beyond Vagermound came a deep "Hallo." The hills played catch-ball with the echo, throwing it around until it was thrown away somewhere in the bottoms.

"Sound like Big Mat!" she cried.

They all sprang to their feet.

"China, you and Melody go hide in the corn crib. That white man jest might be with him—ain't no tellin'."

"Tell him us run off for good and ain't no use

in lookin' for us," called Chinatown as they ran for the crib.

Crouched inside the crib, they sat tensed, bodies and faces slatted by the sunlight hitting through the planks. Just to be hiding filled them with mad-dog terror. Hiding in the red-clay hills was something always in the backs of their heads. It was something to be thought of along with bloodhound dogs and lynching. Chinatown was ducking his head up and down trying to peep out across the yard. The sun and shadow played across his rolling eyes.

Melody had to talk or get out and run away.

"Maybe we hadn't ought to taken that white man's money."

"He give it to me hisself. He give it to me. You seen him, Melody."

"Yes, I seen him."

There was a sound of hoofs in the yard.

"I ain't asked him for nothin'. He give it to me. All by hisself he give it to me."

"I seen him."

Hattie's voice came around the house. "China, Melody, c'mon out. Ain't nobody but Mat."

Chinatown let out his breath. The gold in his mouth laughed.

"Shucks, Melody, if that was that jackleg come back he couldn't handle us."

"If he do come back we make tracks for the hills and then double back to the crib. Be sleepin' while he out lookin'."

They saw Big Mat coming into the yard, leading

a big-boned mule by a rawhide. They ran toward him, Chinatown waving the big-money bill.

Hiding his cheek under one big hand, Mat listened to them tell about the crazy jackleg. Not one muscle in his body moved, though Chinatown was waving the bill under his nose. Hattie was the first to notice his strange calm.

"What on your mind, Mat?"

He took his hand away from his face. A long purple welt blossomed on his cheek.

"Misery! Misery!" wailed Hattie.

Chinatown and Melody pressed in on him with questions. Hattie kept up her cry: "Misery! Misery!"

"Git the stuff packed," Big Mat said. "We goin' to be at Masonville Junction 'fore midnight."

He pushed them aside and started up the big hill that topped the fields.

"I knowed somethin' had to happen," said Chinatown. "When the coot come afore the duck——"

"Lord, what become of us?" wailed Hattie.

Mat stood looking at the fields. He stood a long time. Late evening. The sun was low at his back. His shadow went out from his feet to lie across the land. He felt in his bones that this was his last look at the checkered hills. Never again would the ground be something to work. It was a solemn feeling. He talked it out of himself in what was a prayer.

"Ain't nothin' make me leave the land if it good land. The hills bigger 'n any white man, I reckon.

Take more 'n jest trouble to run me off the hills. I been in trouble. I been born into trouble. Share-worked these hills from the bad land clean to the mines at Madison. The old folks make crop here afore we was born. Now the land done got tired. All the land got tired, 'ceptin' the muck in the bottoms. It do somethin' to a man when the corn come up like tired old gents.

"Somehow it seem like I know why the land git tired. And it jest seem like it come time to git off. The land has jest give up, and I guess it's good for things to come out like this. Now us got to give up too."

At dark they left, and Hattie, barefoot, was in the doorway.

Two

SQUATTED on the straw-spread floor of a boxcar, bunched up like hogs headed for market, riding in the dark for what might have been years, knowing time only as dippers of warm water gulped whenever they were awake, helpless and drooping because they were headed into the unknown and there was no sun, they forgot even that they had eyes in their heads and crawled around in the boxcar, as though it were a solid thing of blackness.

There were so many men in the car that for a long time Big Mat was lost from his brothers. Somebody had started to crawl around in the dark. Soon everyone was moving about. Big Mat had ended in a corner. He crouched there, body shaking with the car. Now and then his head struck against the wall with a noise that was lost in greater noises. His big muscles cried out for movement. Warm urine began to flow into the corner where he sat. He did not move. He was in misery, but his misery was a part of everything else. The air, fetid with man smell and nervous sweat, the pounding of the wheels shaking the car and its prisoners like a gourd full of peas, the piercing scream of the wheels fighting the rails on a curve, the uniform dark—those things were common to all. The misery that stemmed from them was a mass experience. Big Mat could not defend his identity against the pack.

The rattle and jar of the wheels kept Melody from singing, although he was feeling bad and had his box with him. The wheels seemed to be saying crazy things, laughing crazy laughs, trying to draw him into the present, trying to make him crazy like they were. Whatever came into his head was copied by the wheels.

Once he called out: "Big Mat, where you?"

The wheels swallowed up the cry and clicked it out, louder and louder, faster and faster. It made his head spin to try and keep up with the fast-talking wheels. He had to shift to another word in order to keep sane. Soon the wheels had him racing along with the new word. Melody was a sounding board for all rhythms. If it had not been for Chinatown and what he said, everything might have become mixed up with those crazy wheels.

Chinatown was sitting shoulder to shoulder with Melody. His grinning jaws ached with the effort of holding his teeth clamped tight. Every time he dozed off the jar of the car would begin to bang his teeth together. Painfully he dozed and started awake. After a while the fear of dozing began to work in his head. He was the first one in the car to crack up. Melody forgot himself, in trying to comfort his brother. The noise of the car was deafening, but they put their cheeks together, and each yelled in the other's ear.

"Ascared to sleep—ascared to sleep! Car shake so it liable to knock the gold tooth right outen my head. Can't lose that tooth—can't 'ford to lose that tooth. Now I go to sleep, and maybe it gits knocked out. . . . Ascared to sleep, and I tired. . . . I tired. . . ."

"Whoa now, whoa, boy!" Melody calmed him like he would an excited mule. "We be outen here 'fore long."

"I tired and can't sleep. All my life I think 'bout a gold tooth, then I gits one. Now maybe I go to sleep, and it gits knocked out. Somebody steal it sure if it gits knocked out."

"Sure, boy—whoa, boy!"

"It gittin' loose now. You kin feel it. Feel it."

Melody put a shaking hand on the tooth.

"It feel all right, China."

"You ain't foolin'?"

"Naw, boy."

"It ain't even loose?"

"Naw, boy."

"You a good kid, Melody," said Chinatown, greatly eased. "Reckon this damn rattlin' an' all drivin' me off my nut."

"That's it, boy—that's all to it."

"You know me, Melody, since I a little rhiney fella. Little Chinatown then. Now it's Big Chinatown. Never was nothin'—still ain't nothin'. But nobody treat a nigger like he got to git tired sometime."

Melody tried to quiet him again. "Sure, boy, I know how it is."

"Yeah, but you got your box to sit with. Everybody call me no-good nigger. Boss man walk by when he ain't got nothin' for to work. When there a job he kicks me if I slows and calls me a no-good nigger. All that make a man feel like he ain't nothin', and a man got to have somethin' he kin grin a little to hisself about."

"Sure is so, boy."

"When I jest Little Chinatown I seen the way things is an' I know I got to have somethin' to make me feel like I somebody. So all the time I dream 'bout a gold tooth, shinin' an' makin' everybody look when Chinatown smile."

"Sure do shine, China."

"Reckon it do. Work for that tooth when all I wants to do is laze in the sun. But that's all right—I gits the tooth. And I jest got to have that tooth. Without it I ain't nobody. Now everybody turn and see who it is when Chinatown smile."

"Sure do, China. Sure do, boy."

The train gave a lurch. They were pounded against the wall.

"Watch out for me, Melody. I do something for

you sometime. Keep talkin', so's I won't go to sleep. Sure as I do I git to boundin' and knock out this here tooth. Somebody steal it then sure. Can't 'ford to lose this tooth. I ain't nothin' when I loses this tooth. I tired—tired. . . . But you and me keep talkin', Melody—keep talkin'. . . ."

Riding away from the hills they were born and raised on wasn't easy. Riding with the rattle of wheels in their ears when they were in the dark, not knowing where they were headed, wasn't easy. It was enough to make them all brittle. Melody knew that. He knew that later on Chinatown would not want to think about the crazy secret things he was saying then. . . . But the shiny tooth did not drop out, and Melody was glad. His brother's voice was the only sound, outside of the wheels, that was real.

When the car finally stopped for a long time and some men unsealed and slid back the big door they were blinded by the light of a cloudy day. In all their heads the train wheels still clicked. Their ears still heard the scream of steel on the curves. Their bodies were motionless, but inside they still jerked to the movement of a bouncing freight car.

A brakeman had to rouse them. "C'mon, stretch your legs on West Virginia ground, boys. Tomorrow you'll be in Allegheny County."

the great shovel had

Three

THEY HUNCHED against one another, whispering and wondering, and big drops of rain, grayed with slag and soot, rolled on the long wooden bunkhouse. Passing the makings back and forth, they burned cigarettes until their tongues felt like flannel in their jaws. There was a crap game going on in the bunkhouse, but the newcomers didn't have any money to put on the wood. There was nothing for them to do that first day, except smoke and keep walking the rows of bunks. Windows stretched in the long wooden walls around them. And outside they could see the things that they would see for a long time to come.

A giant might have planted his foot on the heel of a great shovel and split the bare hills. Half buried in the earth where the great shovel had trenched were the mills. The mills were as big as creation when the new men had ridden by on the freight. From the bunkhouse they were just so much scrap iron, scattered carelessly, smoking lazily. In back of them ran a dirty-as-a-catfish-hole river with a beautiful name: the Monongahela. Its banks were lined with mountains of red ore, yellow limestone and black coke. None of this was good to the eyes of men accustomed to the pattern of fields.

Most of the crap shooters had been in the valley a long time. Some of them took time from the game to come back and talk with the green men.

"See them towers? That's where I works. The iron blast. Don't take the blast if you kin help it. It ain't the work—it's the head blower. Goddamn tough mick. Why, I seen the time when the keeper on my furnace mess up the blast, and the furnace freeze before you know it. That head blower don't stop to find who the fault go to. Naw, he run up and right quick lays out three men with a sow. One of the hunkies yanks a knife on him, but that hunky gits laid out too. I reckon somebody woulda got that mick 'fore this. Only a man ain't much fer a fight when he's makin' four hundred tons of fast iron from one sun to the other."

The men from the hills were not listening. They were not talking. Their attitude spoke. Like a refrain:

We have been tricked away from our poor, good-as-bad-ground-and-bad-white-men-will-let-'em-be hills. What men in their right minds would leave off tending green growing things to tend iron monsters?

"Lots of green guys git knocked out by the heat—'specially hunkies. They don't talk nothin' but gobbler talk. Don't understand nothin' else neither. Foreman tell one old feller who was workin' right next to me to put leather over his chest. Foreman might jest as well been whistlin', 'cause when the heat come down there that hunky lays with a chest like a scrambled egg."

Yes, them red-clay hills was what we call stripped ground, but there was growing things everywhere and crab-apple trees bunched—stunted but beautiful in the sun.

"Them old fellers hadn't oughta be put on a furnace. Course, a green man got to expect to git pitted up some. Lots o' young'uns got lead in their pants, and they gits tagged when the flame come jumpin' for their shovel. There always burns, too, when the furnace gits tapped and the slag spills over into the pit. But the quicker a man learn to move around on his feet the longer he stays livin'."

A man don't git to know what the place where he's born looks like until he goes someplace else. Then he begins to see with his mind things that his eyes had never been able to see. To us niggers who are seeing the red-clay hills with our minds this Allegheny County is an ugly, smoking hell out of a backwoods preacher's sermon.

"Mebbe they start you new boys out on the skull buster. That's a good way to git broke in. But jest keep minded that you got to be keerful o' that old devil, skull buster. Kill many a green man.

How? Well, magnet lift the steel ball thirty feet
up and drop her. Steel ball weigh nigh eight tons.
That eight tons bust the hell out of old scrap metal.
Got to be keerful not to git some of it in your
skull. Yessir, many a green man long gone 'cause
he couldn't keep old skull buster from aimin' at his
head."

*What's the good in strainin' our eyes out these
windows? We can't see where nothin' grows
around here but rusty iron towers and brick stacks,
walled up like somebody's liable to try and steal
them. Where are the trees? They so far away on
the tops of the low mountains that they look like
the fringe on a black wear-me-to-a-wake dress
held upside down against the sky.*

"Skull buster don't git as many as whores git.
Roll mill help the gals out. Feller sees all that hot
steel shooting along the runout tables, all them
red-and-white tongues licking 'twixt them rollers.
Feller go hog wild fer any gal what 'll take his
money. She don't have to work him up none—he's
hot from that bakin' steel."

*The sun on the red hillsides baked a man, but it
was only a short walk to the bottoms and the mud
that oozed up between his toes like a cool drink to
hot black feet, steppin' easy, mindful of the cottonmouth.*

"On the floor, under the Bessemers, you ain't got
time to think what a gal's got 'tween her legs. . . ."

Melody and Chinatown went out into the wet.
The door closed behind them. The rain had less-

ened to a drizzle. They could hear the clank of the mills over the steady swish of the rain. Melody led the way. He turned away from the river and walked toward the town.

"Boy, this here North don't seem like nothin' to me," complained Chinatown. "All this smoke and stuff in the air! How a man gonna breathe?"

The drizzle stopped. Thin clouds rolled. Melody looked up. "Sun liable to break through soon."

"Won't make no difference to us if the sun don't shine."

"How come?"

"There won't be no crop to make or take out."

"Sun make you feel better," said Melody.

"Couldn't shine through the smoke, nohow. Long time ago a fella told me a nigger need sun so's he kin keep black."

Melody kicked Chinatown with his knee. Chinatown kicked back. Soon they were kicking and dodging around the ash piles. They were laughing when they came to the weedy field at the edge of town. Both men stopped. The laughter died.

Quivering above the high weeds were the freckled white legs of a girl. She struggled with a small form—a little boy who wanted to be turned loose. Other children were peeping through the wet grass. They began to chant, "Shame, shame! Mary and her brother—shame!"

Chinatown and Melody wheeled and hurried away. They had no need to speak to each other. In both of them was the fear brought from Kentucky: that girl might scream. Back in the hills young Charley had been lynched because a girl screamed.

Breathing hard, they followed the path until it became a dirt street. In front of them was a long line of women waiting in front of a pump shed. A few boys crouched underneath one corner of the shelter, held by a game with a jackknife.

"Look—more hunkies!" breathed Chinatown.

"Keep shut," warned Melody.

The pump at the edge of town watered about fifty families. Every Saturday the women were here in line. This day they carried bathing water home. The rain had soaked into their shawl head coverings. They stood patiently.

Then one of the boys spied the three strangers. He was on his feet in a second.

"Ya-a-a . . . "

A rock whizzed between Melody and Chinatown. The two men halted, confused. In the eyes of all the Slavs was a hatred and contempt different from anything they had ever experienced in Kentucky. Another rock went past. Chinatown started to back away.

"We ain't done nothin'," cried Melody. He took a step toward the pump shed. The women covered their faces with their shawls.

"We ain't done nothin'," he cried again.

His words were lost in the shrill child voices: "Ya-a-a . . . ya-a-a . . . ya-a-a . . ."

Melody backed after his half brother. A little

distance away they turned and trotted riverward.

"So this how the North different from the South," panted Chinatown.

"Musta mistook us for somebody," said Melody.

"When white folks git mad all niggers look alike," said Chinatown.

"Musta mistook us," insisted Melody.

It should have been easy for them to find the bunkhouse. The river was a sure landmark. But, in turning in among a series of knolls, they lost direction and found themselves back at the town. Before them a dirt road ran between rows of frame shacks. A large pile of garbage blocked the far end of the road.

"Oughta be somebody we kin ask where the bunkhouse," said Chinatown.

"Well, I ain't knockin' on nobody's door to ask nothing."

"All we got to do is start back to the river."

"Which way the river?" puzzled Melody, craning his neck around.

The light rain had started again. A mist had arisen through the rain. The low mountains were no longer visible. The mills along the water were blotted out. Their sound seemed to come from all directions.

"Maybe if I climbs that garbage . . ."

Chinatown started at a run down the road. At the top of the garbage pile he got his bearings. To the west the gray was tinged with faint streaks of orange.

"Over yonder apiece," he yelled, pointing west-ward.

At the cry, white faces appeared in the doorway opposite him. Nothing was said. Little faces gri-maced between the overalled legs of the bearded father. With a movement of her hands beneath an apron, the mother fanned the breadth of her hips at him. An old Slav bent like a burned weed out of the window. Great handle-bar mustaches dripped below his chin. With eyes a snow-washed blue, he looked contempt at Chinatown. Then he wrinkled his nose and spat.

Chinatown slid down the pile of wet garbage. Hardly daring to hurry, he walked the middle of the road to the place where Melody waited.

"These here folks ain't mistook nobody."

They made quick tracks in the mud to the west.

At the river they did not stop to rest or look around. They wanted the shelter of the bunkhouse. This new place was full of hatreds that they did not understand. Melody led the way down-river. They had been going ten minutes when he stopped. There was no sign of the bunkhouse. Nothing but the river looked familiar.

"You reckon we been goin' wrong?" asked Chinatown.

"Got to be one way or the other," said Melody. He turned and looked behind him.

A fat-cheeked black girl moved along the river-front road. Bright red lipstick had turned to purple on her lips. A man's hat was pulled down over her ears. She wore an old overall coat over a stained satin dress.

Melody stared at her. She drew the coat tight around her hips and began to swagger. He was drawn by her eyes. They were cold pieces of wet glass.

"Wish I knowed what the way to Kentucky," Chinatown was moaning. He turned and saw the woman. "Man! Man! Kentucky kin wait."

The girl passed them. Her swimming eyes invited. They caught a heavy scent of perfume. Under the perfume was a rot stink. The stink sickened them. They were unnerved.

"Howdy, boys. Green, huh?"

They whirled and faced a small, dark man. He shifted from one foot to the other. His movements were like a squirrel's.

"Howdy," said Chinatown.

"How come you know we green?" asked Melody.

"They give all green niggers the same clothes," said the man.

"Oh . . ." Melody's gaze followed the woman.

"Beside, only a green man stop to look at that there gal."

They questioned him with their eyes.

"Her left breast 'bout rotted off." The man laughed. "You kin smell it a mile away."

"What you know!" Chinatown laughed.

Melody was stunned. He could not get the wet

eyes out of his mind. All he could think to say was, "We lost from the bunkhouse."

"You been goin' wrong," said the man. "Back the other way a piece."

"Obliged," said Melody.

"I got to pass by there. Point it out."

"Obliged."

They walked along together.

"You work around here?" Chinatown asked.

"Blast. Boss of stove gang," said the man.

"Oh," said Chinatown. He looked at the old overalls.

"Sparks," explained the little man. "They'll git you too."

"Oh."

A group of Slav workmen came out of a gate in front of one of the mills. They moved with a slow stiffness, hardly shaking their drooping mustaches. There was dignity in the way they walked.

"Uh-uh," groaned Chinatown.

The workmen paused at the gate. One of them turned and waved at the little black man.

"Hallo, Bo."

The little man waved back. That greeting was the easy familiarity of men who had known each other over a period of years.

Chinatown voiced what was in his mind: "That there's the first white guy we seen don't hate niggers."

Bo asked, "You been havin' trouble?"

"Everybody treat us like poison," said Chinatown.

"Everythin' be smooth in a coupla weeks," said Bo. "Always hate new niggers round here."

"How come?"

"Well, company bring them in when there strike talk. Keep the old men in line."

"Oh . . ." said Chinatown. They walked a little. "There strike talk now?"

Bo looked him in the eye. "Looka here, boy. I don't know nothin' but my job."

"Yessir," said Chinatown.

"Don't mean nothin' by talkin' short," said Bo, "only it ain't a good thing for a feller to go spoutin' off."

"That's like Kentucky," said Chinatown.

Within sight of the bunkhouse, Bo stopped in the open to let water.

"Good idea," he said. "The outhouse always full of flies. Smells because nobody sprinkle ashes like they supposed to." He laughed. "Sometime a lizard use your behind for a bridge when you on the hole."

The men from the hills had always let water in the open. It made a feller feel free—space around him and the warm water running in the weeds. Nothing overhead but what God first put there. This touch of the past relaxed them. Their recent experiences became the unreality. This was the reality. They felt for a minute like Bo was an old friend.

"Well, so long," said Bo. "Be keerful. They puts green men on the hot jobs afore they know enough to keep alive."

They stood and watched him cut across the weedy ground to the cinder path leading to the lunch car.

Back in the bunkhouse. Big Mat, Chinatown, Melody—the Moss boys—walking around in a place so strange that one of them might have been dreaming it for the other two. In the bare boards underneath one of the windows there was a knothole. It had a swirl like the top of an onion gone to seed. To the Moss boys that knothole was bigger than all the steel mills.

Later they were in their bunks but far from sleep. They could hear the noises of the dice game, still going strong. One of the men had told them that the game had been going on for years, the night shift taking over when the day shift was at work.

The Irish foreman broke the noises of the game, assigning the shifts. Most of the new men would work in the yards. A few would stoke the "mules," small engines that hauled steel along the river front.

That word "mule"—it sounded like home.

A shift was anywhere from ten to fourteen hours in the heat. Everybody averaged around twelve hours a day. Knowing that, they should have slept but they listened to the high, whining voice of a crippled Negro called Smothers. One of the men whispered that Smothers was off his nut. Yet they listened and heard a different sort of tale:

"It's wrong to tear up the ground and melt it up in the furnace. Ground don't like it. It's the hell-and-devil kind of work. Guy ain't satisfied with usin' the stuff that was put here for him to use—stuff of top of the earth. Now he got to git busy and melt up the ground itself. Ground don't like it, I tells you. Now they'll be folks laugh when I say the ground got feelin'. But I knows what it is I'm talkin' about. All the time I listen real hard and git scared when the iron blast holler to git loose, an' them big redhead blooms screamin' like the very heart o' the earth caught between them rollers. It jest ain't right.

"So what happen? There a ginny falls when they pourin'—and the preacher got to say service over a hundred tons o' steel. For no reason there's somethin' freeze in the blast furnace. Then it slip, and hot coke and metal rain down through the roof on the fellers round the bosh. Any time you foolin' round fast metal it liable to blow up. It always blow for no reason at all, 'ceptin' it want to. . . .

"Listen close now, an' I'm goin' to talk to you so you know something. Steel want to git you. Onliest thing—it ain't gittin' you fast enough. So there trouble in the mills. Guys wants to fight each other —callin' folks scabs and wants to knock somebody in the head. Don't nobody know why. I knows why. It's 'cause steel got to git more men than it been gittin'. . . .

"Can't blame the ground none. It give warnin'. Yessir, they was warnin' give a long time ago. Folks say one night there's somethin' fall right outen the sky, blazin' down, lightin' up this ol' river in the black o' night. Guys ain't stop meltin' long enough to see what it is but next morning they finds it. A solid hunk o' iron it be, big around as a house, fused together like it been worked by a puddler with a arm size of a hundred-foot crane. Where it come from? Where this furnace in the sky? You don't know. I don't know. But it were a warning to quit meltin' up the ground."

Smothers pulled himself to his feet by taking hold of the bunk above him. His eyes held all the green men until he got his crutches underneath his armpits. Then he shook his head in a last warning and hobbled out like a parched-up hopper-grass.

> *"It ain't quite daylight, but it's four o'clock,*
> *So wake up, niggers, an' piss on the rock. . . ."*

One of the boys woke the green men with that cry. He had done time on a Georgia chain gang. Outside, the light had not pierced the morning smoke cloud. Through the windows the men saw the red ball on the horizon. It was a strange waking to a muted sunrise. It was hard to realize the morning.

Some of the old hands kidded, "You ain't never goin' to work in daylight. Now it too early. Next week you work the night shift, and it too late."

The new men had heard how they changed to the night shift. One crew would have to work twenty-four hours in the heat. That did not mean anything to them now. Now they did not like the taste of the sooty air. They missed the sun.

"Got to blow the chimneys ever' night," they were told.

"When the air gits good guys is hungry," they were told.

Everything was too strange for the green men to comprehend. In a daze, they were herded to the mill gates and checked in. The night shift was getting off. They mingled for a few minutes at the mill gates. All of them were gray in the dirty river mists, but the men who had finished a turn were easy to pick out. Their shoulders sagged as though the weights of their coats were too much. The green men carried overall coats over their arms. They had been told to put something on after a turn, that even on a hot day a guy chills, coming away from the heat. They had on long underwear also. That would be good to take the sweat off when the heat really came down. The men from the hills hated the heavy shoes cramping toes used to gripping the dust.

The Moss boys waited in line with the rest. They

were given numbers and keys to lockers. Their eyes were open, but they were not seeing the mills yet. They did not know how they arrived at the locker room. All around them men were changing into working clothes. The green men were given cold stares. Nobody spoke to them. They sat on a bench at one side.

An open-hearth worker had the locker next to the Moss boys. He was an Italian. Everybody called him Mike. Mike had a good heart. He showed them how to tie handkerchiefs around their necks. He made sure they had smoked glasses and heavy gloves. He warned them to wear two pairs of pants if they were put on a hot job—hot-job men always had a lot of holes burned in their clothes. Mike told them what had happened to him on the hearth.

"So there I, workin' Goddamn number eight. Pete throw switch, and furnace go over." He showed them how far the furnace had tilted, slanting his hands. "Goddamn slag run over at door. Some go in buggy car in pit. Some miss Goddamn slag hole. So sp-t-t-t-t-t-t—I think I Goddamn lucky not get burn bad. One, two, three hour later I standing up between Goddamn furnace catch little sleep. I wake up Goddamn cold. Fellas laugh like hell, 'cause spark burn right round pants top, an' Goddamn pants drop off my behind. Maybe I lucky not get burned, huh?"

The men laughed. Laughing, they broke up in little groups, headed for the places where strong backs were needed to do work too small for the great machines. The Moss boys waited until the call came for the yard and pit men. They slouched along in the gray morning. Big Mat was ahead of his brothers. They had always thought of him as big and powerful as a swamp tree. Now, in their eyes, he was getting smaller and smaller. Like spiral worms, all their egos had curled under pressure from the giants around them. Sooner or later it came to all the green men:

What do we count for against machines that lift tons easy as a guy takes a spoonful of gravy to his mouth? The magnets, traveling cranes and steam shovels that do the loading and unloading—in a week they handle piles of stuff that would keep a crew of a thousand guys busy for months. That charger, for an instance—it fills eight furnaces quicker than it takes the crews to make back or front wall. Them hoppers moving up the side of the blast—they fill it before a guy can get the sweat off his forehead. What does that make a man?

The foreman was telling the green men about the old way of filling the blast furnace by hand. "Guys up on top of the blast didn't have a chance when things went wrong. . . ." he was telling them.

Melody was not listening. Smothers had said that men were making steel. Well, it looked to him more like the machines were making the steel and men just hanging around. One thing he knew that Smothers was right about: everywhere the metal was fighting to get loose. The shaping mills were far down the river, but he could hear the awful screams when the saws bit into the hot metal. The blast was a million bees in a drum. The open hearth was full of agony. The daylight was orange yellow with the droning flames of the Bessemers.

Melody whispered to Chinatown, "Wouldn't surprise me none if the Judgment turn out to be jest a steel mill. . . ." He was not joking.

"Sound like circus animals tryin' to git loose," whispered Chinatown.

To get to the pit they had to pass underneath the hearth furnaces. The foreman led the way under number four. All of the men but Chinatown and Melody got through without difficulty. When they ducked to follow the crew a curtain of fire appeared in front of them. Slag was dripping down through a hole to the floor of the pit, and there was no buggy in place to catch it. A couple of thin branches of liquid fire followed the slag. The branches grew large as a man's arm and flowed into one another. That liquid fire was "fast" steel. It hit on top of the slag and spattered. Chinatown yelled. His clothes began to smoke in a dozen places. They lost no time in getting out of there.

They came through under number five. O'Casey, the little pit boss, was there to give them hell.

"What in blue blazes you guys think this is?" he shouted. "You bastards ought to be docked half pay for takin' your own Goddamn time gettin' here."

"We couldn't git under——" began Melody.

O'Casey left him in the middle of the words. The red face glowered up at the rest of the crew. "What the blue blazes you guys waitin' for? Hop it! Clean up that mess front of number four!"

Half of the cleanup gang was made up of Slavs. They took their time getting to work. They knew that all pit bosses raised hell. It was the thing for a pit boss to do. Big Mat grabbed a pick and was at the slag before they could spit enough to slick their hands. They looked their disfavor. Big Mat would outwork everybody. He would spoil the rhythm of the crew. That would give the pit boss something else to raise hell about. Chinatown and Melody worked with a young Slovac. He wielded the pick; Chinatown shoveled, and Melody handled the wheelbarrow. The pile of stuff they were working on was red hot; its core was still molten. Their feet heated and blistered.

Chinatown said, "When I think how we usta throw wiggle worms in hot ashes jest for fun I feels like crying."

Melody laughed.

"What you find to laugh for?" asked the Slovac. "This three-, four-hour work."

"Sonabitch let furnace go to hell," grumbled another of the men.

"You guys talk too much," yelled O'Casey from across the pit. "Get to diggin'."

"Stuff too hot for pick," yelled the Slovac. He dropped his pick. O'Casey came on the run.

"What the blue blazes!" he cried. "Git back on that stuff!"

"Too hot for a pick."

"You wasn't hired to work in no ice house," yelled the pit boss.

Some of the other men on the gang dropped their tools and backed away from the hot mass. O'Casey looked around desperately for a minute. Then he walked up to the biggest man on the floor of the pit—Big Mat. His head not as high as Big Mat's tobacco pocket, he had to lean backward to look the big man in the eye.

"You big dumb hulk of a bastard," cried the pit boss, "where's your brains?"

Big Mat dropped his shovel and glared down at the pit boss.

"Ain't you got brains enough to know what to do when the stuff is too hot?" cried the little man.

Big Mat opened his mouth to speak, but the words did not come out. His eyes glazed. He stood like a stupid child taking deserved punishment.

"Git the hell over there and find a hose!" commanded O'Casey.

Big Mat trotted away. O'Casey turned to the rest of the gang. His glance flashed over them with new confidence.

"Stand back and wait for that hose! Then hop to it! This furnace's due to pour in a halfa hour."

The men stood back. O'Casey walked to the other side of the pit and expelled his breath in a long sigh.

A couple of the Slavs were too close when Big Mat turned the hose on the hot mass. There was a great hiss, and steam reached out and enveloped the two men. Cursing in their own tongues, they danced a crazy pattern. If Big Mat had not been so big he would have had a fight on his hands.

While the men were grumbling there came a long "Look o-o-o-out below!" Nobody had to tell the green men what to do. They scrambled under one of the furnaces. Maybe a crane had broken, and its ladle of hot metal would come pounding down to destroy the pit. But the danger was not overhead. It was only a spout flowing on number seven. The mud had burned out of the tap hole, and the fast steel was pitting the ground in a bright flood. They had to put on dark glasses to watch it. It was over in a few minutes. The furnace was tilted back so that the flow stopped.

The men who had been grumbling forgot all about Big Mat.

"This is an unlucky day," one of them sadly remarked.

"Don' no sonabitch know how fix spout round here?" screamed the young Slovac to everybody within listening distance.

"My feets is burnin' up," Chinatown said to Melody.

"Mine is hot too," Melody told him.

"Yeah, but if we got to clean up that there steel my feets goin' to git mad an' take me on out of here." He half grinned.

Melody grinned with him. The foreman was sending another crew to clean up the new mess.

They pried up the last of the slag with crowbars. And then there was time to take on a fresh jaw of cut plug. Big Mat went to watch the crew tap number two. Chinatown and Melody went to sit between the furnaces. It was cooler there. Melody took out his sack of tobacco and rolled a smoke. Chinatown got his chew soft and spat a long brown stream against a wheelbarrow. He stretched his arms over his head.

"Guy don't git no chance to sleep round here," he complained.

Later he would know the truth of his words through experience. It would always be time to start back to work before he was completely rested from the previous shift. Then if he went with the other fellows to raise a little hell before turning in he wouldn't get any rest at all.

"Think I knock off a few winks right now." Chinatown yawned.

"Sure, boy. I keep a lookout," promised Melody.

The thanks died on Chinatown's lips. His eyes closed, and he snored easily. Melody did not mind keeping watch. Chinatown was doing well to keep any kind of job. Melody thought about himself and Chinatown dozing in the sun back in Kentucky. The heat of the pit was like the sun at midday. Maybe they were in Kentucky. Maybe Maw was alive and in the back-door garden. Maybe Hattie would come in the doorway and say, "Wake up, you two lazy scapers. Vittles is done." He could not rouse himself, and Hattie was yanking at his shoulder.

It was Big Mat shaking him. Slowly he came to himself. He couldn't remember just when he had fallen asleep.

"Wazza matter?"

" 'Nother cleanup job," said Big Mat. "Pit boss been raisin' hell."

Melody sprang to his feet.

"Pit boss jump on me 'cause you guys ain't around," said Big Mat.

"I think O'Casey got it in for you."

They got Chinatown on his feet. When they joined the rest of the gang O'Casey cursed Big Mat for taking so much time. Then they were hitting the hot slag again. The green men were not in the rhythm of the crew. Their pace was uneven. They grew very weary. There was nothing like working on hot slag for tiring a man, they thought. You worked a little while, and then the needles started all over your back, and you just had to lean on your shovel for a spell. They couldn't understand it. The slag was very light. Maybe it was the heat.

When the foreman told them to go to lunch most of the green men could hardly drag away to the mill yard. Big Mat was untouched by the toil, but Chinatown and Melody staggered as they walked. Chinatown did not want any food. He was too tired for eating. His muscles ached. Tears rolled down his face. Melody thought that all his life he would be seeing curtains of fire flowing down through slag holes. And when he thought about the long day ahead he got sick in his belly.

Three weeks Chinatown and Melody staggered back to the bunkhouse, asleep before their heads touched the bunks. At the end of the fourth week they were able to stay awake and carouse with their fellow workers.

Melody lay on his back, guitar across his chest. Every now and then his hands started idly over the strings but they did not find much music. He didn't try any slicking. That was for back home and the distances in the hills. Here at the mills it felt right to find quick chords with the fingers—a strange kind of playing for him, but it was right for that new place. Later he would take his guitar with him to the Mexican section of the town. Yesterday he had promised a woman a song. She would want to hear a ballad to make laughter— "The Midget and the Knock-kneed Gal" perhaps. She would not care about this new music he was trying to find. His fingers searched, and he watched the game going on in the cleared space near the door.

Among the kneeling men was Chinatown, holding the dice high, praying for his point.

"Ho dice, ho dice," he chanted, "send that

yella money to join his folks. Ha!" The dice clicked for silence and rolled for Chinatown.

Melody saw Chinatown make his point. He put the guitar to one side and took a bottle from under the mattress of his bunk. A big drunken Irishman, standing by the door, saw the bottle and weaved toward the bunk. Melody held out the corn whisky.

"You kin take the spider off."

The Irishman took a little gulp and passed the white corn back. Melody drank deeply. The Irishman took his long drink, and the bottle was corked. With the corn burning down in his guts, Melody took up the guitar and found a little more of the new music. It was nothing like the blues that spread fanwise from the banks of the Mississippi. It was here somewhere in the whirling lights and in the hearts of great red ingots.

But the big Irishman was reaching for the bottle again.

"G'wan, boy, knock out a tune. G'wan . . ."

Melody turned his head away from the red face, and there were Big Mat and Smothers sitting in a corner. Smothers' voice rang above the noises of the dice game, making him forget the drunken slobbering in his ear. He listened to Smothers' words:

"Lawd ain't cuss you like steel cuss you. A guy make money—sure—but it jest fade away. Come Monday, ever' dollar he sweat gone away."

"Send a little to Hattie ever' week," grunted Big Mat. "Put aside a little o' the rest. I got to git a house. I got to send for Hattie."

The big Irishman was leaning closer. Melody could almost taste the tobacco-and-whisky breath.

"Hit somethin' hot on the Goddamn box, boy. G'wan . . ."

In a corner of the room an argument was going on. One of the old hands, Dusty-butt Jones, he was called, waved his bottle and shouted.

"Us niggers was brung here jest 'fore the war," he was shouting. "Iffen they hadn't been fightin' we still be down South makin' crop 'stead o' steel."

"The dumb niggers like you maybe. I'd 'a' left anyhow," shouted back one of the men.

The argument became more and more heated. After a while they had to hold Dusty-butt. He got his name because of his shortness. Men said that the seat of his pants dusted the ground. Yet they had to hold him, or he would have jumped a man twice his size.

Chinatown had his golden grin turned to the roof.

"Hep me, hep me! Come seven! Ha!" There was more yellow money between his knees than he had known was in the world. But he rolled the dice as if it were no more than pitching new coppers of a Sunday.

Smothers had upped his voice to a shrill falsetto. "All these here fellas say jest like you sayin' when they first come round here. They ain't know the cuss o' steel. They all got folks back where they come from."

"Gotta send for Hattie," said Big Mat.

"You never see her again," shrilled Smothers.

Dusty-butt was angry because the men had held him from a fight. He looked over at Smothers and grunted.

"Don't leave that crazy bastard talk on you," he told Big Mat. "How the hell he know anythin'?"

"How I know anythin'?" cried Smothers. "How I know anythin'?"

"Yeah, how you know anythin'?"

"Same way I know dead men's voices in chains and plate. Same way I hears bridges talk in the wind."

A spasm of laughter broke open Dusty-butt's mouth, and nobody could hold out against the laughter. It swelled among the men.

The Irishman was excited by the noise.

"Hit them strings, boy!" he howled into Melody's ear, and began to shuffle.

The laughter still swelled. The drunk was disgusted with Melody. He started away. Then, to point up his disgust, he flung back over his shoulder: "Sure, you're a hell of a nigger."

The boards under the Irishman's feet made loud cries in the suddenly quiet room.

Chinatown held the dice motionless above his head. He was kneeling stiffly over his money. The black men in the room looked out of the corners of their eyes. A couple of whites, standing by the door, kept their heads down. Everybody was waiting for something to happen. Melody was waiting for something to happen. He was supposed to do something but he couldn't think what to do. A couple of slow seconds passed. Then Big Mat got up and moved to the side of the bunk.

The Irishman swelled. He swelled his neck and moved nervously over the creaking boards.

"Wot the hell! Wot the hell!" he muttered under his breath.

Big Mat did not seem to know what to do.

"Leave him be," he said.

"Wot the hell! Wot the hell!" chanted the drunken Irishman. He looked all mixed up. Perhaps he didn't even remember calling the name that had lifted every black face in the room. Perhaps he did not know that at the mills "nigger" passed only between black men. He was backing out fast. He was running from the pressure of eyes.

"Wot the hell!"

And he was gone.

Big Mat looked around. With one hand he made a little sign at Melody.

"He don't play so good," he grunted. "Jest make the music what in him."

The dice began to click in Chinatown's raised hand. The clicking lost itself in the noises of men talking and laughing.

Big Mat stood there by the bunk for a long time. Melody would have spoken to him if he could have thought of something to say. By the look on Big Mat's face, the bunkhouse had disappeared, and his thoughts were sunk deep in his head.

It was not long before Chinatown made the throw that put him out of the game. A thousand dollars had passed through his hands. Now he was broke. Lighthearted, he came over to Melody's bunk.

"Let's git out and have some fun," he cried.

"Whyn't you quit when you had all that yeller under you?"

"One frogskin just like the other when you gamblin'."

"Yeah, now it's have some fun on my money."

He laughed and pulled Melody off the bunk by his legs.

"Somewhere there's gals and a moon strong enough to throw a shadow, and you talkin' 'bout whose money belong to who."

While Melody was getting on his shoes Chinatown went over to talk with Big Mat.

"Melody and me goin' out to git some bitches."

It took a while for Mat to answer through a nod of his head.

"We git some more whisky too," said Chinatown.

"Yeah," he grunted.

"What's the matter with you?" asked Chinatown.

"Nothin' the matter."

"Seem like you been polled in the head with a ax handle."

"Jest makin' out to think."

"What about?"

"Got to send for Hattie. This here a good place to be at."

Smothers broke in. "All my talk wasted. I think I got somebody who listen when I tell the truth. Steel fool you and kill you."

"Shut up!" Chinatown laughed. "That there's gobbler talk."

Smothers drew himself up, and Chinatown had to stop laughing.

"I been round here a long time. The mill take my legs." He took up his crutches and hobbled out.

Chinatown looked as sheepish as a grown man could look. He kept his eyes on Smothers' stiff back until the little man passed through the bunkhouse door.

"Sonofabitch, he git touchy of a sudden."

A lot of the men had been drifting out of the bunkhouse. The corn whisky was giving out. All of them stayed full of the stuff from the time they got off until they were checked in at the mills again. Of course the hot-metal workers had to keep liquored up. There was always a craving in them that wasn't to be satisfied. Even when they had all they could drink their insides still felt parched.

"C'mon, China," called Melody. "The whisky

be all gone, and the gals be all taken 'fore we git there."

"Jest tryin' to see if Big Mat go along with us."

"Mat never go anywhere—you know that," Melody told him.

"C'mon, Mat, have a little fun," coaxed Chinatown.

"Savin' my money to send for Hattie."

"What do a few dollars matter?" asked Chinatown. "You drive yourself crazy sittin' round here all the time."

"Hattie there waitin'."

"Man, you don't know what a woman like till you see them gals at the cat house."

"My woman waitin'."

"Everythin' go here," said Chinatown. "The gals come down from Pittsburgh for the week end. Anything you pick——"

"Naw."

"C'mon, China," called Melody.

"Hattie ain't gonna like it around here nohow," said Chinatown.

"Gotta send for her," droned Mat.

"She ain't gonna like wearin' shoes."

"She's gonna learn."

"She ain't gonna like cookin' on no stove."

"She learn."

"Aw hell!" said Chinatown. "If you wants to drive yourself crazy, sittin' round all the time, well, that's you."

Melody tucked his guitar under his arm, and they left Big Mat.

They were already full of liquor but they went to the line of one-room shanties where the Mexicans sold themselves for a dollar if the buyer would take some green corn whisky.

There were dogs everywhere. Stray curs came smelling at their heels. They did not kick at them. The whores of Mex Town had more love for animals than men. One steel worker who had killed a dog had been found on an ash pile. A knife had let his blood soak the ashes.

After one visit Chinatown and Melody had known just about every woman in this part of town. They were liked because they brought laughter. That meant a lot in a place where big red and black men made steel twelve hours in every twenty-four.

Only a couple of lamps were burning in this part of town. They went into the first lit-up shack. Two women were seated on the bed. One was heavy hipped and fat breasted, stringy black hair falling in lines over her khaki face. They knew her. She was called "Sugar Mama." They had never seen the other woman before. She was something to look at. Her face was broad as a spade but good to see. The eyes were big and set even with her brows. Her hair started almost at her brows and was like a live bush. She looked good because she was young. Most of the women around here were washed out and hard used. Else, why should they have to wrestle with mill hands?

"Ah, my friends!" yelled Sugar Mama.

"Mama, you ol' 'gator!" yelled back Chinatown.

"It is good you are here." She turned to Melody. "And you have bring the guitar like you promise."

"Can't play yet," he told her. "First I got to get drunk."

"*Sí, sí*, everything go better when men get drunk." Sugar Mama laughed. She reached underneath the bed and pulled out a bottle of something. Melody drank deep and passed the bottle to Chinatown.

"Where everybody around here?" asked Chinatown between gulps.

"They come back soon enough," said Sugar Mama. "Everybody is go to see the dogs fight."

"Lawd, I clean forgit they was pittin' the dogs tonight!" said Chinatown.

Melody had forgotten too. He was looking at the broad spade-flat face.

"We still got time to make it, Melody," said Chinatown. He set the bottle on the floor.

"Naw."

"C'mon, we take Mama and the other one with us."

"I could not go," said Sugar Mama with a sigh. "I must stay here with this sick one."

"Oh, she sick," said Chinatown.

"Yes, she is a new one. I send for her. I pay railroad here. I think she bring many men in the house. Now she sick, and it is Friday."

"Who is she?" Melody wanted to know.

"Anna, she is called."

"Who is she?" he asked again.

"She is my niece."

"Ain't nothin' like keepin' business in the family." Chinatown laughed.

"That is what I think," said Sugar Mama. "But now she is sick. And it is Friday."

"What the matter with her?"

"She is a no-good one—lazy. . . ."

" 'The work ain't hard, and the boss ain't mean,' " sang Chinatown.

"You are a funny one—*sì*." She poked her elbow into his ribs.

"You are a funny one—*sí*," mocked China, and tickled Mama on her fat backside.

Sugar Mama shied away and giggled.

"You see, I tell her the men not bad. But no, she is here three days, and this one hurt her, and that one hurt her——"

"Maybe they did hurt her," said Melody.

"But she is acting the new one," said Sugar Mama. "And already she bring a baby into her mama's house. The papa for the baby is four, five, six fellow—maybe more."

The girl was not looking at anybody in particular. Her eyes were fixed on the opposite wall. There was no expression in her broad face. She didn't seem to care that she was being talked about.

"She is lazy," said Sugar Mama. "So lazy that up her food comes as soon as it goes down."

"Well, let's git onto the dogfights," said Chinatown. "C'mon, Melody."

"Naw!"

"Aw, c'mon!"

"Take Sugar Mama. I'll stick around here."

"You waste your time," said Sugar Mama. "She is a sick one."

"That ain't nothin'," said Melody.

"She is no good to sleep with."

"I ain't aimin' to lay her."

"You sleep with Mama, *sí?*"

"Naw."

"Well, let's git on now," cried Chinatown.

Melody took out his money and gave half of it to Chinatown. Sugar Mama's eyes followed the green. Then she walked over to the girl and spoke rapidly in Spanish. The girl gave no sign of hearing. Sugar Mama turned to Melody.

"I tell her you are a nice man. She do what you say, or I break her head in. Sick or no sick, it is Friday."

"Sure, sure," said Chinatown. He took her by one of her fat arms and pulled her out through the doorway.

Melody could hear him laughing and hurrying Sugar Mama down the dirt road. The girl shook her head when Melody turned and held out the bottle

to her. He stood there drinking, feeling the corn
fire burning in his guts. Every now and then his
stomach rolled, and he belched. Then the hot
breath of the corn was sickening.

He began to feel at a loss. He couldn't study out
the feeling that made him pass up the dogfights to
stay here. There was a lot about himself that he
would never be able to study out.

The girl helped him.

"The guitar—you carry it for nothing?"

"Naw, I play on it most times."

"You can play a Mexican tune?"

"Maybe so."

"Maybe so?"

"I plays anythin' I feels like."

"Then play Mexican tune."

He sat down and tucked the box into his stomach.
He had to take another drink, because his fingers
couldn't find a chord.

"Don't know how to start, I guess," he told her.

She began to hum something that might have
been a song. All he could feel in her humming was
a rhythm that halted and hopped and halted and
hopped. He shook his head.

She laughed.

"Where is the place you come from?" she said.

"Kentucky."

"I come from Vaughan in New Mexico. It is
not like New Mexico here."

"Reckon not."

"In New Mexico there are goats."

"I seen goats, all right," he told her.

"There I milk the goats and play in the sun all day with the children."

"You mean, when you jest a kid," he said.

"All the time," she said in a clear child voice.

He looked at her again. She did have the body of a woman.

"How old are you?" he finally asked.

"Now I am fourteen, I think. Maybe fifteen."

"You ain't knowin' for sure?"

"I know for sure I am an old one not to have a yardful of little ones and a man sleeping in the sun."

"Yeah?"

"So it is all the same." She shrugged.

He took another pull off the bottle and found himself hitting the guitar lightly. There was a faint smell of cedar in the air. The girl moved closer to him and drew her knees into the rig of her arms. Her dress slid away from her legs and bunched around her thighs. She had legs beautiful as fresh-split cedar.

"What is it you play?"

"Don't know."

She looked up at him and laughed softly. He forgot about her legs, because there was something like a dream in her eyes set even with the brows in her broad flat-as-a-spade face.

"You love me, yes?" she said.

"Sure," he told her.

He was on the edge of something more satisfying than thinking about the quivering snakes her fresh-split-cedar legs could become under his weight. He was on the edge of something but he slipped away. Maybe he was drunk, he thought. The corn in him was powerful. He tried to steady himself, as though balancing something on the end of his nose. It was a chunk of the night, and he had to hold himself steady so it would not fall off.

"You love Anna?"

"Sure, baby."

If he could keep the thing balanced on the end of his nose maybe he would find out something.

"Shame!" she scolded. "A little of a bottle, and you are too drunk to love Anna."

"Naw, I love you," he heard himself saying.

She took his hand off the strings of the guitar and drew it down on her thigh. There was not much feeling in his fingers. Everything was like eelskin.

"Anna love you."

All of a sudden the thing on his nose fell back into his eyes, and through the half-dark he saw her as though she had a new face. His hand came back and ran over the guitar. He didn't exactly hear what kind of music he was making but he knew what passed in his head. This girl had more than one woman shackled in her eyes. All the women he had seen were here. Here was the fat-cheeked black girl he had seen walking in the rain, the woman whose left breast died and rotted until she stank so no man would buy her for a dime. Here, quivering above the high weeds, were the freckled legs of the bohunk being covered by her brother. Here were women smelling of rut and sweat and some of milkweed crushed in the field ground under their raw buttocks, the blues singer in a Kentucky jook joint, lifting her skirt to cover coins on table corners, spreading herself before the boys, crying: "Throw your quarters! Throw a bull's-eye and git it free!" Here were the women seen through a window or behind a door . . . again the sick eyes of that fat-cheeked girl walking in the rain—dead, swimming fish eyes telling a lie. . . . Come lay your floating head on a beautiful-as-fresh-split-cedar belly and let your toes tickle the stars. . . .

Anna spoke in a high, whining voice, and what she said was a cold wind clearing his head.

"You a sissy feller, I think."

"What you say?"

"You got plenty money."

"Yeah."

"Still you play music instead of making love with Anna."

"But ain't you sick, like Sugar Mama say?"

"Bah!" She spat violently. "That's for that old nanny goat. I do not like to see the dogs die."

"But she say you got hurt," he stuttered.

"Nobody hurts Anna, and she is not sick."

The cold wind was still blowing.

"When I turn the trick that fat she-devil takes away the money."

He was seeing with everyday eyes.

"I will not draw the men here for nothing!" she screamed. "I stay like I am sick until she drops dead from men bouncing on her fat belly."

He felt as though he had told this girl something she had no business knowing about.

"When she is dead, then Anna take all the money."

"Yeah, yeah," he said.

She grew suddenly quiet and gloomy.

"But she will not die. She is a tough old bitch, that one. Anna will be old and wrinkled when that old one is holding up a lamp in the window. I never will wear high-heel shoes on my feet, I think." She held out her bare feet for him to see. "I think I am grand in shoes with the very high heels. Never have I had them but sometime I will kill the old bitch and keep all the money to buy them."

"Yeah, but they put you in jail," he said.

"That is right. I guess sometime I get a man who will make love all the time and spend his money for high-heel shoes and grand things."

"Guess you will."

"He will be a big man with muscles like a bear on the mountain. That is so he can kill Sugar Mama if she try to hold me when I go with him. He will have a pine tree on his belly, hard like rock all the night. He will get me high-heel shoes with bright stones in the heels."

She took his hand and put it on the thick bush at her thighs. The cold wind had stopped blowing, but still he didn't want this woman. He felt as

though he had had her already. How he could feel
that way he couldn't figure out.

"You will give Anna money and not tell the old
nanny goat?"

"Sure, sure."

The bottle was almost empty. He finished it in
a gulp.

"Git some more," he told her, waving the empty
bottle.

She fell back across his lap.

"First we make love?" She smiled.

"Naw," he said. "Git a bottle."

"No." She pulled his head down.

"Git a bottle," he said against her lips.

Rolling out of his lap, she hit the floor with a
thud and was on her feet.

"You are a sissy fellow!" she screamed.

Getting up slowly, he took a couple of dollars
out of his pocket and threw them on the cot.

"Them two bucks is to leave me alone," he told
her . "All I wants is corn."

He knew the corn was kept underneath the cot.
She did not move to get a bottle.

"What's eatin' you?" he said.

She was trembling. He could see anger jerking at
the little strings around her mouth.

"What's eatin' you?" he said.

Still she just stood, looking hell at him.

"What bullheads is bitin' you? Ain't you got
your two bucks for nothin'?"

Those words were high wind in a grass fire.

"You pay money not to make love with Anna. Anna would sleep with pigs sooner than you. She would lick the mess off their bellies sooner than kiss you. You are not a man. You squat down to pee. Nothing but a little string hangs from your belly. . . ."

He couldn't do anything but stand there with his mouth open. The stream of words had knocked him out on his feet.

"You are a sissy feller."

"Now wait a little while——" he began.

"Get out, sissy! Get out!"

"I ain't no sissy," he said.

"Get out," she screamed at him, and broke out cursing in Spanish. In the middle of her cursing she turned and started to run out the back door. Before she had gone more than a couple of steps she came back and snatched up the two bills. The door slammed after her.

There was nothing for him to stick around for, he thought. He would go back to the bunkhouse and try to sleep. After all, tomorrow was Saturday and the long shift. He would need that sleep to stand twenty-four hours in the heat.

Saturday morning Big Mat went to the mill a changed man. A-borning in him was a new confidence. He did not sink into himself when O'Casey singled him out as scapegoat for the mistakes of the crew. He looked the little pit boss in the eye. O'Casey knew men. He knew when to let up. The other men were quick to sense the change. They passed little looks among themselves when O'Casey passed by Big Mat. They began to lag in their work. The pit boss had to do something to save face. Luckily, one of the pouring crew failed to show up. And when the call came for a replacement O'Casey recommended Big Mat.

Bo had said that they put the green men on hot jobs before they knew enough to stay alive. That was true. Black George, one of the men from the red hills, had been slow learning. They had put what was left of him in the ground. But Big Mat proved to be a natural hot-job man. After the first turn he did not have as many burns to grease as had the regulars.

The steel pourers' shelf was just a narrow platform high up against a wall. Around it was a rickety iron railing. Big Mat was told about that railing. One of the pourers said, "It was jest put up lately. 'Fore that a guy who faints rolls right into heaven."

They did faint on the shelf—especially on hot spring days like this one. But Big Mat welcomed the heat. Through the long, hot hours he would do twice as much work as anybody else. In competition with white men, he would prove himself.

The Bessemers were directly across from the shelf. Through the blinding heat Big Mat saw them in a haze—the blower on the pulpit, watching the tall air-stretched flames, the flaming air pulsing through the white metal, shimmying thirty feet above the live steel, blowing at the sun through holes in the roof. Once Big Mat had thought the holes were there so the flames could light the sky at night. Once the drone of the Bessemers had frightened him. Now his ears did not hear the drone. The steel began to blow noiselessly after he had been a short turn on the shelf.

The blower was an old Irishman. He knew by the color of the flame when it was time to tip a Bessemer. Now he waved his gloved hand at the shelf. Someone let out a warning "Hallo-o-o-o-o-o!" Big Mat followed the example of the men around him and yanked down his dark glasses. The Bessemer sighed, and the place was full of sparks. The furnace was tilted. And almost before the full ladle could move on its overhead tracks to the pourers' shelf another great Bessemer went into its noiseless song.

Hollow molds were moving beneath the shelf. The pourer signaled when the first was in position. He pulled the lever on the full ladle, releasing the white fire. Through his glasses Big Mat could see the red winking eye growing in the bottom of the mold. The stream that fed that eye threw off curtains of sparks, pinpricking his hands and face. He got his signal and threw strips of manganese into the glowing mold. He was continually dodging, but still the sparks fried in the sweat of his chest where the leather apron sagged. The red stream stopped suddenly. Another mold slid underneath the ladle.

Without slowing between molds, they took tests of the steel. The sweat ran into Big Mat's wide-mouthed gloves and made small explosions when it fell on the hot test steel. Big Mat did not flinch. Alone he held the spoon steady. It took two hunkies to hold up a spoon. He smiled behind his expressionless face. His muscles were glad to feel the growing weight of the steel. The work was nothing. Without labor his body would shrivel and be a weed. His body was happy. This was a good place for a big black man to be.

Melody and Chinatown were helping on the floor underneath the Bessemers. Naked to the waist, they worked hard, cleaning a big ladle for relining. The air was stifling. When Melody raised his lips upward to search the thin air he could see Big Mat high above. Pushing up his glasses, he wiped the sweat out of his eyes. He could see the liquid steel hitting the sides of the test spoon, scattering in clouds of white stars over Mat's gloved hands. Even to his hazed eyes, Mat's muscles sang. His own muscles did not sing. They grew weak and cried for long, slow movement. He could not stop them from twitching. It was not the heat and work alone —the rhythms of the machinery played through his body—the stripper, knocking the hardened steel loose from the molds. He couldn't hear it. It would have been a relief to hear it. He felt it inside himself—the heavy rhythm of the piston that used only a stroke to a mold. That rhythm in his body was like pounding out those ingots with a blow of his fist. And he was tired. Twenty-four hours had to pass before he could stagger away to the bunk-house. Only a thought kept him on the job: next week end he would pleasure himself in Mex Town while some other bastard was baking on the long shift.

Chinatown was inside the big ladle. He could see the sun lancing through cracks in the ceiling high above. The heat of the sun sitting on the roof was nothing to the temperature inside the ladle. But it was just that little added heat that was too much for him to stand. His clothes were wet to his body. Where he squatted there was a wet spot. He was being smothered in a blanket of heat that pressed in from all sides. His lungs ached for mois-ture. He would have killed somebody for a drink of water. Yet there was water not far away. He had been told not to drink his fill. They had told him to put a tablet of salt on his tongue. The salt was crusted in his throat. He climbed out of the ladle. O'Casey saw him start for the hydrant.

"Just rinse out your mouth and spit," warned O'Casey.

Chinatown fastened his lips to the spigot and turned the water on full force. His lips still clung when the foreman pulled him away. They had to take him out in the yard to untie the knot in his stomach. Then he was sick. Never before had he been so sick. Inside himself he prayed to die if he ever felt like that again.

Between spells Melody and a gray old Slav came out into the yard to watch over Chinatown. The old man's name was Zanski. He looked over the dozing Chinatown to Melody's drooping shoulders.

"You ain't feel so good either?"

"Head turnin'," said Melody.

"Maybe you hold your head far down to the ground . . ."

Melody tried it.

"Do kinda help some."

"Make heat drip out through head."

"Obliged."

"All feller work in heat know that."

They didn't say any more until it was almost time to get back to the floor.

"Sooner be shot in Kentucky than do another turn," groaned Melody.

The old man smiled.

"Don't nothin' git you guys?" asked Melody. "You jest work and work till it git discouragin' to watch."

Zanski pushed his beard away from his lips and gestured at the two men.

"Colored feller alike. Work in mill but ain't feel happy."

Chinatown raised himself on one elbow. He looked at Zanski and scowled.

"Heat liable to git anybody," he broke in defensively.

"Not heat."

"Well, what then?"

"You fellers don't move out of bunkhouse. You got no kids."

"Jest don't want none," said Melody.

"You got no woman. Feller ain't be happy like that."

A thought of Anna flashed into Melody's head. He said nothing.

Chinatown said, "That's where you wrong. You ought to see them boys headed for the cat house of a Saturday."

"That ain't woman."

"You got to git in line for them whores."

"That ain't woman."

"Line reach clear round the mill, I betcha."

"That ain't woman who keep white curtains in a feller's house. Whore girl ain't wash curtains."

Chinatown was puzzled. He did not know what Zanski was talking about. To cover up he said, "Yeah, and they'll roll you if you ain't slick." He settled back to doze again.

The old man went on, "Feller from Ukraine workin'. His woman wash the curtains, and the kids growin' in the yard."

"Hundred o' them," said Melody, because that was the way it looked on washdays.

"Them kids work in the mill sometime. Their kids grow in the yard."

"That makes you feel happy?" mused Melody.

"I think about that when the heat comes," explained Zanski.

"That wouldn't help me none," said Melody.

The old man was silent for a time. Then he spoke as though he knew more than was in a barrelful of books.

"Feller from long way off die like plant put on rock. Plant grow if it get ground like place it come from."

Melody felt the words. But talk faded into nothing in the face of the heat. Under the Bessemers he sweated and gulped the thin air. In his body played the noiseless rhythms of the mill. Before morning he was so worked up that his voice was high and thin, like a knife running over an E string in his throat.

It was seven o'clock when the Moss boys got to the bunkhouse. There was a letter waiting for Big Mat. He stayed awake to read it. But Melody and Chinatown were like dead men. They were so full of little needles that they had trouble remembering their own bunks.

Almost before they closed their eyes it was time to go back to the mills. Every Monday after the long shift it was the same. They had to drink almost a pint of corn whisky to give them heart for another shift. Chinatown and Melody shared a bottle, but Big Mat did not need the stuff. He was ready to go, so they took a last drink and followed him toward the mills.

Chinatown's eyes were red rimmed. The whisky was burning in his eyes. Melody, too, was shot through with the stuff. Yet they were sober. Sometimes steel workers were sobered by the foggy evening. Away somewhere in the fog was the clank and pounding of the plate and sheet mills. Chinatown gave a quick shudder, like a mule shaking off flies. Melody remembered the time he had pulled a mole out of the black, cool ground into the bright light. Chinatown's shudder brought back that mole and the way its dead eyes feared the sun.

"Don't like it," muttered Chinatown.

Melody did not answer. He felt what Chinatown meant.

"All the time my body jumpin' like hell," cried Chinatown.

"Keep shut!" rumbled Big Mat.

"Down home I be catchin' the last sun round 'bout now. Onliest time I move be when the shade move."

"Mill your home now," Melody told him.

"Mill never be my home," he said.

Melody turned that over in his mind. Someday the mills would be his and Big Mat's home. Mat had faced a mick who said the word that passed only between black men. Back in Kentucky everybody had called them "nigger." It was something for Mat to have so soon unlearned that. He himself had unlearned a lot of things. The old music was going.

Now when he took down his guitar he felt the awe of a night—white with leaping flames. Sure the mills would be their home. But the mills couldn't look at China's gold tooth and smile. In the South he had worn that tooth like a badge.

If China had a chance to work a hot job it would be better for him. That would be something important. He could wear a scorched, spark-pitted face. He could wear that face like all hot-metal men wore it—that face was a badge. The hot-metal men had to wash in kerosene, come Saturday. The smell of that kerosene stayed with them all week. That was a badge too.

Before they got near the office, to check in, the fog parted and was whipped by the sun's last long lashes. Those same lashes fought the fire in the mill chimneys. The fire was driven back into its sooty holes. The fading lashes hurt their eyeballs. They walked along, squinting under their hands.

Suddenly Big Mat reached into his pocket and drew out a crumpled letter. He thrust it at Melody. There was enough light in the leaden day to read by, but Melody had to strain for the crabbed print. Chinatown started to look over Melody's shoulder but he was not seeing the letter. His eyes were trying to focus the shadows underneath the dresses of two Slav girls caught against the sun. Melody poked his ribs.

"Don't want to read it," said Chinatown. "Jest tell me what it say."

Melody looked at Big Mat. His face was heavy

as always. The heavy skin on his forehead was bunched with the effort of thinking. He was not going to speak.

"It tell about Hattie," Melody said.

"I never knowed Hattie could write," said Chinatown. "She musta studied up fast."

"She git this writ for her," growled Big Mat.

"What the writin' tell?"

"She fall and lose the baby," said Melody.

"Whose baby?"

"My baby," said Big Mat simply.

"Oh, she was gittin' ripe afore us go away then," said Chinatown.

"I knowed it happen," said Big Mat.

"Maybe it ain't certain," said Melody.

"Naw," grunted Big Mat, "she only carry it this long so the curse be harder to stand."

"The curse oughtn't work in this new place," said Melody.

"They all git dropped dead."

"Make me crave more corn to hear a man talk that-a-way," said Chinatown.

"Mat, there ain't been no curse here, fer as I kin see," said Melody.

Big Mat stopped and looked up at the towers of a mill in their path, the dirty orange of the hearths, the violet gas flames ghosting the air above a bunch of tall chimneys. There was a hot-wool-on-his-chest feeling as foundrys breathed around him. He jerked his thumb to take in all those things.

"Got so this seem better 'n farming to me."

"Yeah," said Melody, to keep him talking.

"I kin stand up to a man and outwork him."

"Yeah."

"So I forgit all 'bout the curse."

"Yeah."

"Now another time my woman slipped her baby."

"Here's corn ready to make you forgit it," said Chinatown. And he pulled out his bottle and took a long pull.

"All this time I ain't got drunk once," said Big Mat.

"You wrong, 'cause corn and fast gals change your mind," said Chinatown between gulps.

"Ain't had no woman."

"Them gals in Mex Town change your mind quick," said Chinatown.

Melody said, "Keep shut, China!"

"I oughta preach the word, but the word ain't in me to preach."

Melody tried to comfort him. "The word in you, Mat."

"I think maybe if I be a good man I lose the curse, even if the word ain't in me."

Melody could see the hurt in the boot-leather face. He could sense the big fear that the long, tough muscles couldn't fight. Maybe Chinatown was right. Sometimes corn whisky could wash the lump out a guy's throat and make his fears things to be handled with his fists.

"A little corn won't hurt one way or the other," he told Big Mat.

"Now you talkin' business," cried Chinatown.

"Hot-metal man ain't due to be sober," said Melody.

"C'mon, Mat," begged Chinatown.

Big Mat shook his head.

"Well, they pittin' dogs again," said Chinatown. "Let's go after we do this shift."

It occurred to Melody that Anna would be at the dogfight. He became enthusiastic. "Jest to the dogfights, Mat. It do you good—keep you from thinkin'."

"It ain't nothin' bad," said Chinatown.

When Big Mat nodded his head Chinatown grinned in delight.

"When I die don't bury me," he sang. "Jest pour me back in the jug."

A couple of helpers had failed to show up on the open hearth. The boss melter on number six told Big Mat and Melody to work the hearth until the regular men were sober enough to come back to work. Melody didn't like the idea but he kept his mouth shut. A boss melter was not the man to take any back talk on Monday.

This Monday had done something to every man in the mills. There was trouble starting. Men were strung high, like the strings on Melody's music box. These Monday mills hit bad chords, and every man was ready to lay his buddy out at the wink of an eye. One of the Slavs let a hot test block fall. It crushed the toe of the Italian working next to him. The Italian was screaming as they took him away to the hospital. He was screaming that the Slav had done it purposely.

The accident cleared the air of tension for a while. Everybody but Big Mat talked and laughed as though it were a joke that a man got a toe mashed. Chinatown and Smothers came to the hearth.

"I don't suppose it make you mad if you smashes a toe or something and has to lie up between sheets for a couple of weeks," Melody said to Chinatown.

"I hear they gives you a big dose of croton oil every day you in the hospital," said Chinatown.

"That the truth," said Smothers.

"How you know?" asked Melody.

"Fella name of Jones was up there," said Smothers. "When he leave his guts hang out clean to the ground."

"How come they do that to him?"

"Nobody likes that," said Smothers. "So whether you is well or not you come on back to work—which is what they want you to do."

Chinatown opened his mouth and let out a guffaw. It exploded from so deep in this throat that he had to feel to know if it loosened his gold tooth.

"What's funny?" asked a young Irishman who

was knocking off a little time from his control
levers.

"Jest thinkin' 'bout a guy I hear went to the
hospital once. They give him croton oil every day
for a month. When he come out he so cleaned out
that when he open his mouth the wind whistle
right through him an' make a noise like a bugle."

They all laughed like madmen. All the hearth
crews began to laugh. There was laughter in them
that might turn into screams as wild as if they had
smashed toes. Smothers was the only one not laughing.

"Who was that guy?" he asked.

"It don't matter—he dead now." Chinatown
laughed.

"What he die of?"

"Hurricane came along and blew him inside
out," howled Chinatown.

The hearth rocked, but Smothers did not crack
a smile.

"That too bad," said Smothers. And the hearth
was wild with laughter.

The boss melter was letting them carry on as
much as they pleased. The laughter was loosening
up the men. Men who were ready to hop at each
other's throats a moment ago were slapping each
other on the back.

At last the boss melter had to send them back to
work.

"Get the hell off the hearth!" he told Chinatown
and Smothers. "Beat it before I lay you both out."

He gave them a friendly shove, and they went down the iron steps to the yard.

"C'mon, boys, c'mon. You number-six crew—back wall."

They hopped to the job.

There was rebuilding of the furnaces—back wall and front wall. Test the metal and get a jigger of steel to thin it out. There was tapping all along the hearth and remudding of burned spouts. There was fine hard coal in bags to be flung to the full ladles—also magnesium. There was the fearful heat and men with quivering muscles, trying to live through another Monday on the hearth.

O'Casey came within a hairsbreadth of not living through this Monday. The men were brittle again, and O'Casey slapped one of the hayseeds in the face. They called all the young white fellows who were Americans and new to the mills "hayseeds." And this hayseed had it coming to him. He had missed a test block with a sledge, and the hammer had come down on the concrete. O'Casey, on his way to the pit, had gotten the flying concrete in the face. Any worker might have hit the hayseed for something like that, but the hayseed held anger in himself until the heat brought it to the surface. Later, when everybody had forgotten about the slapping, the hayseed grabbed a shovel and tried to use it on O'Casey. Big Mat saved O'Casey's life. Before the shovel could come down through a short arc he had laid out the young hayseed. They were taking his limp body away when the men got the call to lunch.

Chinatown, Melody and Smothers ate their lunch together. Zanski came and told them what "fella do" Monday night after a long shift has left them like walking dead men.

"Steel lay off, and fella lay on," said Zanski. "Always like that."

"I ain't layin' on nothin'," said Chinatown. "My back broken from the pull of that damn barrow."

"Steel do seem like it tired, of a Monday," said Smothers, "tired of yowling. Guess men got to yowl then, got to run right at each other's throats."

"Whisky, whores and wheelbarrows," chanted Chinatown.

"Ever notice how mean the foremans git of a Monday?" said Smothers. "Fella jest can't do nothin' right for them."

"The mick with my crew say I got to keep up, or he put me with the shovel crew in the coke yard," said Chinatown.

"Take the hayseed get himself laid out on job," said Zanski. "He work side to side of men maybe three week. He ain't talk to nobody. Then come today. It Monday, and O'Casey get concrete dust when hayseed miss block. If it any day but Monday hayseed still on job. He never go off his nut 'bout little slap. But it is the day it is. So he laid up in company hospital with big pain where Big Mat have to hit him. Maybe tomorrow mornin' he ain't know why."

It came time for them to go back to work, and they went. The time between spells for the men on the hot jobs seemed to get shorter and shorter as the shift wore on. The twelve hours into Tuesday sunrise were worse than the twenty-four hours of the long shift. Sometimes men went crazy from thinking ahead of the hot work to be done before they could stagger out in the cool morning and bathe their heads in the water trough.

Now it was six-thirty Tuesday morning. The hell was over, and men gathered around the trough to soak their heads and talk a little. They talked about the trouble at the hearth. Big Mat was the hero of the morning. Everybody agreed that it was a great thing he was quick enough to knock the hayseed out before O'Casey was hit. Because of this praise Big Mat did not come near the trough.

A big Irishman who was boss melter in charge of five furnaces told Melody:

"Never had a colored helper work better on the hearth. He's strong as an ox—do everythin' the melter tell him to do and take care of the work of a whole crew if he ain't held back."

"He's got some Irish in him somewhere." Another red Irishman grinned. "Lots of black fellas have got Irish guts."

Still another red face and reddish head blew under water and came out shaking like a setter dog and talking about Mat.

"That black fella make a whole lot better Irisher than a hunky or a ginny. They been over here twenty years and still eatin' garlic like it's as good as stew meat and potatoes." He glanced sharply around to see if any of the foreigners had heard him. There were none at the trough. They didn't have much to say to anybody. They had left for their courtyards.

O'Casey walked up to the trough. Taking up his pail and overall coat, he grinned the length of the yard at Big Mat, who was leaning against a pile of steel plates left to age and rust a bit in the weather.

"Black Irish—that's what he is," said O'Casey.

Chinatown came up to the trough in time to hear what was being said.

"That there's my brother," he cried proudly, his fixed grin taking them all in.

O'Casey waved across to Big Mat.

"So long, Black Irish," he called.

Big Mat did not answer. He was full of savage pressure. The thought of the dogs tearing at each other was pleasant.

The dogfights were held in an old barn away from the town. Sometimes when the weather was good they held the fights in open fields. There were men around here who raised dogs for nothing but fighting, and some who brought their dogs from as far away as Altoona and Harrisburg. A lot of money would change hands. Steel men had saved their money for this moment. Today a man had brought a bull terrier all the way from Akron. That bull terrier was unknown around these parts. His owner had offered to pit him against any dog of near weight and take all bets. Perhaps that man had not heard of Son, the police dog that had beaten every other dog within a hundred miles.

Son's owner was old Bob Dank, who knew how to keep a dog savage and ready for blood. Bob Dank kept Son in a dark closet for weeks at a time, feeding him raw meat sprinkled with gunpowder. Sometimes old Bob would let him out and tease him with a sharp stick. Son would tear up anything that came within the radius of his chain.

Chinatown and Melody were full of corn whisky. Their money was on Bob Dank's dog. They had seen Son fight and knew that he would let nothing live, once he had tasted its blood. Chinatown had forgotten everything in the excitement of the evening, but Melody kept Big Mat in his eye. Big Mat had not bet anything on the fight. He stood around the pit with the rest of the sweating mob and waited for the dogs to fly at each other. Melody didn't know whether or not Mat was going to like it. There was nothing to give him a clue. But away in the back of his mind was a memory of Big Mat tearing a mule's life out with a sharp rock. That was a memory to make him uneasy. He did not know what effect the sight of violence would have upon his brother, to whom violence came as a thunderblast.

The barn was full of people in a sweat to smell hot blood. Soon Melody was lost from Chinatown and Big Mat in the milling crowd. When the fight started that crowd would go into a solid, quivering mass of hard faces, mouths slobbering in eagerness for a kill. When that happened Melody could go away to a corner and wait. He didn't like anybody to know about it, but when the people got like that and an animal was dying he had to turn away or vomit. For him, though, there was something else in a dogfight. He came again and again to feel the lives of these people burning together in a single white flame. That flame acted on like him like whisky, and he burned with it.

The same folks came to the dogfights again and again. He knew a lot of people in the crowd. Somebody was slapping him on the shoulder every few minutes. At every slap he called out the same greeting and kept moving. Finally there was a tug on his arm and a familiar greasy smell. He turned and faced Sugar Mama.

"Ah, my friend!" she cried. "And where is the yellow one?"

"Who you talkin' 'bout?" he asked.

"The grinning brother who tickles Sugar Mama and laughs always."

"Oh—Chinatown. He's around layin' more bets."

"You are betting then?"

"Sure."

"You are betting much money?"

"Week's pay," he told her.

"*Sí, sí,* that is good. You will win and come to Sugar Mama's house."

"Maybe."

"Maybe—maybe." She nudged him in the ribs. "Maybe you will see somebody. That one who was sick is not sick again. You like her?"

"Anna?" He said her name and felt as though he had confessed something that had been on his mind a long time.

"Anna is that one. *Sí,* I think she is crazy about you." She nudged him again.

"Aw, stuff!" he said.

"No—no stuff. She does not say so, but she not can fool Sugar Mama."

"Aw . . ."

"She is here," said Sugar Mama. "I will get her. You wait—you wait."

Sugar Mama was off. His eyes combed the crowd for her. He felt a little sad, because he knew what would happen when he met Anna. In his mind she had been something that her body could never equal.

But the handlers of the dogs, red stained, padded gloves protecting their hands, were ready to turn their fighters loose. The bull terrier was standing quietly, like an old warrior saving all his strength for the fight to come. Son, the police dog, was raging and twisting to cross the pit to his calm foe. He was raging and twisting, and old Bob Dank was feeding that rage by slapping a peppered and raw-meat-scented glove across the dog's nose.

The fight was on, and from the first the men who knew dogs saw that Son did not have a chance. Son was a good fighting dog but he was up against a champion. A lot of folks in the crowd didn't know that. They were yelling because Son was putting on the best show. They did not see that the bull terrier was playing a waiting game, waiting for Son to tire and leave the throat unguarded for just one vital moment. That moment was bound to come and in twenty minutes it came.

Son raged in and slashed at the bull terrier's hind legs. By just the foam on his jaws he missed hamstringing his enemy. The terrier whirled and dived at his throat. Son was too tired to spring away. He crumpled under the weight, and his throat was hidden between grinding red jaws. The fight was over.

The crowd was silent, so that the sobbing breaths of the women became a roar. The fight was over, and a lot of men had lost money, but there was no thought of money at the kill. Nobody expected old Bob Dank to step in and save his dog. A dog once beaten like that would never fight again. But Bob Dank's cry rang out:

"Haul him off! Haul him off!"

The dogs were doused with cold water and pulled apart. Bob Dank lifted a heavy stick in his hands.

"I want to kill this no-good sonofabitch myself," he cried.

Every eye was on the club waving high in the air. Then a woman darted forward. It was Anna.

Bob Dank knocked her back with a blow between the breasts. Before she could fall Big Mat had jumped into the pit. One swing of his arm sent Bob Dank halfway across the barn, knocking people down like straw stubble. Everybody knew by Big Mat's eyes that he had gone hog wild. Son, bleeding and shaking, got to his feet and charged. Mat's booted foot swept upward, and the dog's lifeless body spun into the surging crowd. Then hell broke loose.

Melody didn't know just how he got out of the barn. Maybe he was carried by the crowd that was scattering like chickens before Big Mat's fury. He stood outside in the gathering evening and pressed against the side of the barn to keep from being knocked down by the ducking figures. He stood there until everything was quiet. Then he peeped through the doorway. There was Big Mat, limp in the center of the floor, and Chinatown dancing around him.

"Boy, that was some fight! Boy, did you see me? I got two at once. . . ."

Big Mat was drooping and bewildered.

Chinatown cried, "This action done give me a thirst. I think I'm dried out again. Let's us git some corn and celebrate. C'mon."

He led Big Mat outside. Mat came easily. Before they had gone more than five steps a woman rushed up to them. Anna. Melody reached for her, but she threw herself on Big Mat and kissed him on the mouth. Chinatown pulled her away, and she ran across the field like a crazy thing. Big Mat stood shivering in the leaden evening.

The Moss boys walked the dirty string of river front. Melody sang a dirty ballad. Some of the verses he had heard; some he had made up. Chinatown harmonized with him on the familiar verses.

Big Mat followed a step or two behind them. He had followed them through the town, in and out of every "corn joint" they could find. One gulp after another had funneled through his throat, and still the look on his face was the same as when Anna had kissed him. His shuffle was even and sure.

"He a born drinker, as sure as God love Sunday," sang Chinatown.

Maybe it was Sunday, thought Chinatown. The gals were still on their front porches, knees close together to hide what was beneath their cotton-print dresses. As they passed Chinatown sang the dirty songs louder and tried to see what the women were doing. Most of them stared at him from some unheard-of distance away. A few grinned and pulled at their short skirts.

"Should of brung your music box along," he told Melody.

"Might of got busted in the fight," said Melody.

"These here bohunks ain't appreciatin' us singin'," said Chinatown. "Oughta have music along with it."

"Maybe we ain't singin' so good."

"What they know 'bout singin'?" he said. "Never hear 'em sing a note."

Melody looked at him, surprised.

"Them foreigners sing good."

"Hell, they don't sing nothin'."

"What they do then?"

"Yowl is all they do," he said, "and a man can't understand one word they yowlin'."

Melody had heard some of these people from the Ukraine singing. He hadn't understood one word. Yet he didn't have to know the words to understand what they were wailing about. Words didn't count when the music had a tongue. The field hands of the sloping red-hill country in Kentucky sang that same tongue.

"I like hearin' them yowl," he told Chinatown.

"Aw, shucks, Melody"—he laughed—"you kin even hear music in a snore."

Melody laughed and turned to see if Big Mat was going to laugh.

"I kin hear music in a snore," he repeated.

Mat's eyes were on the shacks. He seemed only with them in body. Melody wondered if Mat's mind was with his eyes, stripping the print cloth off the pale, freckled Slav girls on their porches.

"Boy, look at Mat," he whispered to Chinatown.

Chinatown did not look around.

"Aw, he ain't never laughed in his life."

"Naw, look how he givin' them gals the eye."

Chinatown saw and whistled softly.

"After all the time he been holdin' hisself in, I feels sorry for the first gal he grabs."

Mat stopped as a little girl, no more than ten years old, came out of an outhouse behind one of the shacks. Her pants were still down in back, and she was carefully holding her dress high. Melody and Chinatown stopped to watch Big Mat.

Out of the back yard next door came a gang of little towhead boys. They saw the girl and turned into hunting dogs circling something they had flushed out of the brush. Too late the little girl saw them. She darted for her doorstep, but they had her. Without a sound she went down on her back, fighting silently. Twisting and turning, a furious little figure was dragged away to the tall weeds up the riverbank. The weeds tossed violently and then trembled for a little time.

"Can't see why she don't yell some," said Chinatown.

Melody knew she could not have yelled out. It was a game they played. Or, better, it was a thing they did that was no game but had rules like a game.

Big Mat's eyes were fishskinned. He started to walk on. Now Melody could see that he was drunk —drunker than any man had ever been before. Melody thought he was drunk like this long before the corn went into him. The corn just let the drunk show in his eyes.

Boys were playing ball in the dirt road. The path was blocked but only for a short time. Legging it down the road was one of the little hunters they had watched a short distance back.

"Hey, guys! Hey, guys!" he was shouting.

The ball game went on.

"Hey, guys, they linin' up on ol' Betty back in the weeds!"

In a confusion of thudding feet the road before them cleared. Balls and bats were dropped. A string of shavers legged it back to line up on ol' Betty.

Chinatown watched them go and laughed long and deep.

"She jest a few years older and have a coupla more pounds round her belly, and I'd run to git in that line myself."

"Aw, c'mon," said Melody. He started on.

Big Mat was standing as though he would never move again.

"C'mon, Mat."

"Look like Mat ready to git in that line right now." Chinatown laughed.

"C'mon, Mat," Melody called again. "We go on down the line to the Mex shacks."

"Better 'n that, ol' Betty got some big sisters down from Pittsburgh," said Chinatown. "Onliest calling card you needs is green money."

"Naw, we make Mex Town," Melody insisted.

Big Mat turned toward them and suddenly he was sick. Corn whisky was bad coming up. They knew how that felt. Chinatown jumped out of the way, because Big Mat didn't bend over like a sick man does. Big Mat stood straight up, and the liquid gushed out between his teeth like a river at flood.

"Git low to the ground, Mat! Git low!" cried Chinatown.

Big Mat stood upright until the last of the stuff had run down his chin and into the front of his open shirt.

"The word never be in me," he muttered in his wet lips.

They were ready to hold his head or do something for him. He was off before they could approach.

"Where you goin' to, Mat?" called Melody.

Big Mat strode on, and they had to trot to keep him in hearing of their voices.

"Wait up, Mat!" Chinatown was calling.

"Wait up, Mat!" Melody heard himself.

They passed the pump at the edge of town.

"There some water to soak your head, Mat," cried Chinatown.

But Big Mat did not wait for anything. He strode through the leaden evening, shadow-black until the lighted bunkhouse windows held him in outline. They followed him over a hill and did not call any more.

Walking right through the crap game by the door, Big Mat made for his bunk.

"Hey, look where you goin'!" cried one of the gamblers.

"Look out, Black Irish!" called the man who was holding the dice.

"It's Big Mat," cried somebody. "He's jest broke up the dogfights. Now he's feelin' good. Now he's raisin' hell."

"Old Bob Dank got two broken ribs and a dead dog," yelled the gambler. "He left town."

"Sonofabitch! He better watch where he steppin' or he find out this ain't no dogfight," snarled one man, sucking a crushed finger.

They trailed off into silence. Every eye was on Big Mat. With steady strength he ripped off his filthy clothes. Then he was naked before his bunk. A man napped on top of the thin wool blanket. It was Smothers. Perhaps he had fallen asleep, waiting his nightly talk with Big Mat. Without a word Mat put his arms under the mattress and lowered it to the floor. Smothers was not even jarred. Naked, shiny with sweating, looking like a furred animal come in out of the wet, Mat fell face downward on the steel springs of the bunk. The springs jerked him up and down for a little while. There was no other movement.

"Wot the hell?" breathed the gambler.

One of the men turned to Chinatown and Melody.

"What happened to him?"

"Corn juice happened to him." Chinatown laughed.

The gambler stared at Big Mat and then pointed below the bunk.

"Looka there!"

"Gawd, wot a whopper!" said a man.

The men began to laugh. The room rocked with heavy laughter.

The laughter woke Smothers. He looked around, rubbing his crazy eyes.

"Listen when I say what's in me to say," mumbled Smothers, and he went back to sleep.

Four

Anna had said:

"He will be a big man with muscles like a bear on the mountain. That is so he can kill Sugar Mama if she try to hold me when I go with him."

Big Mat was like that and more. He had handled a barn full of men at the dogfights. He had said things to Anna with his body. Anna could understand. She had seen him in action, traveling back double a thousand years and more to the time when men said things in the talk of the wild beast. So she had talked back in his language. And what she said was all in a hard, quick kiss and a crazy flight across the open fields. Maybe she knew that Big Mat would come for her. He came. And Sugar Mama would have been a dead one if she had tried to stop their going.

Anna had said:

123

"He will have a pine tree on his belly, hard like rock all the night. . . ."

One kiss in an open field. Mat had not forgotten. Two nights in a row he had stayed with her at Sugar Mama's shack. When he took her out of the place and rented a shack they were together every night. For a full week he laid off from work, and Chinatown and Melody did not see him. The shades at the new shack were drawn all the time. It was funny to Chinatown, and he made a joke of it, but Melody did not sleep well. He was full of misery that couldn't be joked away. There was no joke stronger than the thought of Big Mat lying a full week next to her love-scented body.

Anna had said:

"He will get me high-heel shoes with bright stones in the heels. . . ."

So Big Mat came and got all the money he had been saving. Anna went into the stores and came out with rhinestone shoes and dresses like the hostesses wear in the dance halls. The rhinestones did not glitter after one trip down the slushy road. The dresses were heavy around the bottoms where they dragged in the mud. Still, Anna wore her new clothes every day and paraded through the Mexican part of town like an overseer's wife.

It had rained the day Big Mat came back to the mills. The rain had puddled the ground, and already a thin layer of soot floated on the water. He was going to work the night shift. Melody was just going off after twelve daylight hours.

They met in the mill yard and stood a few minutes in the hot wind from the hearth. Mat had been drinking. There was the look about him of a man traveling on whisky instead of muscle. His hair was matted, and matted in it were white threads of cotton—threads from a torn mattress.

With his eyes Melody had searched Big Mat. He did not look like the strong brother from the red hills. He felt a rush of feeling for Mat heat up his face. He wanted to put a hand on him and say something good for him to hear. Nothing could get past a fence between them. There was nothing to do but be casual, half strangerlike.

"How they goin', Mat?"

"Hallo, Melody."

"What's doin', Mat?"

"Ain't nothin' doin'."

"You lookin' good, Mat."

"Ain't feelin' so good."

And Melody had to pick up the talk before it dragged further.

"Fellas all miss you roun' the bunkhouse, Mat."

"Yeah?"

Melody tried to smile and laugh a little.

"Don't know what to do for a strong guy round the place now."

"Yeah."

They couldn't find anything else to say right away. The silence grew painful.

"How China gittin' on?" blurted Big Mat.

"He doin' all right, I reckon."

"That's good."

"Oh, he been a little sick. Too much corn last night."

"That's bad."

"Yeah."

They shifted their weight around to break the muddy cinders in a small circle.

One of the pit men passed and called out:

"Better shake it up, Black Irish. The pit boss full of hell tonight. Had his gal out, and somebody got him drunk and borrowed her for a little while. He'll be mean."

"Well, so long," said Melody.

Big Mat waited for a long second.

"Say, Melody," he muttered, "you don't think —that I ain't—doin'—— That is—that I ain't actin'——"

Melody waited for him to break the thing between them. But Mat's voice trailed off, and they were back where they started.

"Well, so long, Mat."

"So long. . . ."

Melody was all mixed up. He stopped by the railroad lunch car to think things out. He ordered a cup of coffee to sharpen up his thinking.

There was a new waitress behind the counter— straw hair and fish belly white like the other Slav girl that used to sling the food across the counter. A wad of gum popped in her jaws. Because she was new all of the men who came in kept up a constant chatter for her benefit. It was hard to think, with all of the talk going on. He sat three full hours and got nowhere with himself.

Back at the bunkhouse, Chinatown was cleaning an old .22. He was going to take pot shots at the scaly-tailed rats that scampered around the ash piles. He spat on the oiled stock of the rifle and rubbed it in with the heel of his hand. Melody was close before he took notice.

"How they git along without me today?"

"I seen Big Mat," Melody told him.

"Naw!" He laughed. "So the ol' boy decided he got enough at last!"

"Enough of what?"

"Enough of young stuff." He winked. "Mat ain't no chicken no more like he was."

"China."

"Yeah?"

"What you reckon goin' to happen out of all this? What you reckon?"

"What I reckon what?"

"This Mex gal and everything."

"Aw, stuff!" He laughed. "That ain't nothin'. We been tellin' Mat he had oughta loosen up."

"Yeah, but this here different."

"How different?"

"Well, it ain't like jest goin' out to raise some hell with the gals. This here is like he married or something."

Chinatown looked serious for a second, then he poked Melody with an elbow.

"Naw, you jest too young to know 'bout these here things," he said. "A man gotta do what devilment in him—that's all."

There was no use talking to Chinatown. He did not feel like Melody. All of his life he had been around Big Mat, and they had never been much more than faces to each other.

Melody tried again. "China, you know what you tell me once?"

"I say lotsa things once."

"We was walkin' down the river-front road—you, me and Mat."

"So what I say?"

"You say somethin' like, 'Big Mat ain't never laugh in his life.' You 'member? It was jest after the dogfights."

"Boy, that was some dogfight! I got two guys at once—two of 'em—and Big Mat have his back turned."

"Yeah," Melody broke in, "but, like I was sayin', you was right. Things is a joke a lotsa times to us but things ain't never a joke to Big Mat."

"Man and sweet Jesus!" Chinatown laughed. "I never forgit how them fellas scamper when us start turnin' out that place."

"So this gal, Anna, ain't no joke to Mat neither," Melody continued.

Chinatown was laughing.

"Them guys sure lit for the tall weeds. You'd

of thought the devil show up at prayer meetin'."

Melody gave up and began to roll a smoke. Sitting there on the edge of his bunk, he smoked and thought about Hattie back home in the doorway. To him she was still in the doorway, and it was early spring. He thought about her, and Chinatown's chatter was like the smoke in the air around his head. He ought to write Hattie a letter about it, he thought. He couldn't make up his mind, so he said the thing aloud.

"Maybe I ought to write Hattie a letter about it."

Chinatown touched him on the leg.

"I forgit," he said. "There a letter for Mat. It's on his old bunk. Come from Kentucky."

Melody ran to the bunk and picked up the heavy envelope. He knew it was from Hattie.

"What you goin' to do with it?" asked Chinatown.

"Give it to Mat."

"But he at the mill."

He reached down and pulled Chinatown. Chinatown stood up, grunting with unwillingness and cramp.

"Take it easy on a sick fella." He grinned.

"We goin' to Mat's shack and wait for him," said Melody. "We wait all night maybe but we got to talk Mat out of what he's doin'. He got to send for Hattie."

"Aw, stuff! Mat's all right."

"C'mon," he said, and started through the doorway.

Chinatown caught him outside.

"Ain't no use in us runnin' up there right now," said Chinatown. "Mat ain't there."

"We goin' now," he told him. "If I lays down it be time to go to work 'fore I git up again."

Dragging his rifle, Chinatown followed. Somehow Melody hadn't believed his own reasons for going directly to Mat's place. Still, it didn't seem possible that he would want to see Anna. Suddenly Chinatown's rifle cracked. Melody almost jumped from under his hat. Turning, he saw Chinatown grinning and blowing down the barrel of the gun.

"Got that sonofabitch," Chinatown yelled. "Got him with his head in a old tomato can." He spat.

Anna saw them coming. She was at the door. Already she was walking on the sides of the shoes and she still had on the dance-hall dress. It was fuzzy and wrinkled now, but out of the sagging straps her shoulders rose like soft words from loose, bearded lips. She held her ground at the door, looking at them as though she knew they had come evilly.

Waves of heat beat them through the half-opened door. They could see the oil stove behind her. It was red hot. It was like coming up behind the open hearth during a heat.

"Hallo," said Melody.

Anna looked past him and did not say a word. He had to follow her eyes to know that she was fearful of Chinatown's gun.

"He shoots at scaly tails," he told her. "He hate them."

"Got one with his head in a old tomato can." Chinatown grinned.

"Leave the gun go," he told Chinatown.

"Somebody might steal it," argued Chinatown.

"Leave it go, I say."

Chinatown leaned the rifle against the doorjamb and grinned at Anna.

"We come to wait for Big Mat," he told her.

"He go to mill," she said. "Mat work the whole night at the mill."

Chinatown pulled at Melody's arm.

"Aw, c'mon! We can't wait all that time for Mat."

"Naw, we waitin'," said Melody. He pushed past her. Chinatown followed.

Anna closed the door. Her back against it, she watched them as they sat down on the cot. Under her eyes they could not keep their hands and feet still. After a little Anna left her place at the door and sat on the edge of a chair, her hands folded in her lap.

The room was too hot to breathe in. Melody did not complain. The tension left his body. Satisfied, he stole a look at her every now and then. Her broad, flat face expanded. It grew to the size of the room. He was very drowsy.

"Where do Big Mat keep his corn?"

Chinatown was looking around as he asked the question. There were not many places corn could be kept in the one-room shack. He looked around until it became plain that Anna was not going to answer.

"Man, the heat goin' full blast"—he laughed— "but there more chill in here than outside." He looked full at Anna and laughed again. Chinatown's laughter was always good to hear.

Anna had to warm to Chinatown. Nobody ever stayed inside himself when he laughed. She got up and went out the back door. She came back with two milk bottles full of corn whisky.

"This for you," she said to Chinatown, and set the bottles and one glass in front of him.

"Don't you want none, Melody?" asked Chinatown.

"Naw, I ain't drinkin'," he said. "Not until I see Big Mat and say what I got to say."

"Aw, stuff!" he growled. "C'mon, git a glass."

"Naw."

Chinatown started to drink all by himself. One glass of corn in that hot room, and his mouth loosened and sagged. He forgot Melody dozing stiffly at his side. He forgot Anna. Suddenly he began to recite the verse that one of the men had brought from the Georgia chain gang.

"It ain't quite day, but it's four o'clock,
So wake up, niggers, an' piss on the rock."

Anna laughed. That started Melody to laughing a little. Laughing loosened them. Talk started. Anna and Melody did not talk to each other. Each of them talked to Chinatown. In a short while the talk stopped, because Chinatown fell asleep. A long time passed. Chinatown began snoring.

Melody was very still, struggling to keep his eyes open. Little beads of warm sweat formed on his face and tickled as they rolled down the collar of his jacket. At last he had to move. He jumped when his body touched the cold of his sweat-soaked shirt. Anna had pushed off her shoes and pulled the skirt of the long dress up to her knees. He could see the tawny shine on her bare legs. She felt his eyes on her and dropped her skirt. She tucked her feet out of sight.

Then, without knowing why, he felt like saying something that would make her angry, make her do or say something to show herself a little Mex whore.

"I got a letter here from Big Mat's wife," he blurted.

She turned very slowly.

He couldn't stop himself. "Big Mat got to throw you out and send for Hattie."

Her eyes got big in her damp face.

"He read this letter and throw you out," he whispered fiercely.

She said nothing.

He wanted crazily to make her yell, curse and call him names. The letter was in his jacket pocket. He yanked it out and shook it.

"He read this and send for Hattie. He throw you out."

With a snarling noise she came close to him and

snatched the letter from his hand. He grabbed for her arm and held her from the open flame of the oil-stove. She was wild and strong. He had to wait a long time for her strength to break before he could get to his feet without losing the hold on her wet arm. They fought without a sound, locked in each other's arms. Her hands were behind his back. It took all his force to keep her from getting a grip to tear up the letter. They swayed over the table and then moved away. It was as though both had the same desire not to wake Chinatown.

Even while he was struggling Melody's mind went back to the little hunky girl coming out of an outhouse, fighting as she was dragged away to the tall weeds. She had not made one sound. Anna fought, and there was no sound but her sobbing breath.

Close to each other, they strained until he could feel his muscles trembling. He was getting weak and must give up. Suddenly she went limp against him. Off balance, he swayed. She was making no effort to stand by herself. They swayed forward and fell together. She was underneath. He put out one arm to break his weight. The letter was loose in her hand. He was not trying to take it back. He did not know what he was trying to do but he felt her body quivering under him. He felt the arm she clamped around his neck. He saw her free hand reach up to turn out the kerosene lamp.

He did not know when he began to hear Chinatown's slow snore again. Lying on his side, he listened to the soft sound and saw the changing shadows that the oilstove threw onto the ceiling. Under his outstretched arm Anna was quiet and limp. He was resting for the first time in a long while. He did not think about what had happened. He did not think about Big Mat. He lay stretched like a satisfied animal, a long, lean dog that this day has killed a deer.

Later Anna began to talk. She spoke in a whisper, her voice so low that he could hardly hear. This is what she said:

"All the time I am not in Vaughan. Sometimes I am in Mexico with my old people. They are very old, but I would like to be with them. The young fella in Mexico do not pay for love. They come in from watching the goats and digging in the fields and they do not give me money. There is a baby in my mother's house, but that is nothing. My mother will keep the little one, and I will not marry with fella who has no house and watches the neighbor's goats for his bread. All the time I am barefooted, and my mother and my old folks are barefooted. The peons are all barefooted and do not even have white bread to eat. There are many cars pass with *Americanos*, and the cars stop sometimes, and the men have cameras and take pictures of the goats and peons. The women in the cars wear shoes with high heels. The *Americano* get many things for the women. And so I say that I will not marry with the fella who has no house and watches the neighbor's goats. He cannot buy shoes with high heels. All the time I dream of high-heel shoes with bright stones in the heels that will make me like the *Americanos*, and nobody will take my picture along with the goats.

"One day Sugar Mama send for me. She tell me I make plenty money from the *Americanos*. She tell me I make enough money to have high-heel shoes and go to Mexico and be the finest woman in Mexico City. She tell me that I will be finer than the *Americanos* who ride in the cars. So I come to this place. But that old she-devil goat take all the money and do not let Anna keep out one little piece of money even. I do not have shoes. I look like the peon, only there are no goats around the house. I do not mind the men bouncing on my belly. That is nothing, for I look for one big strong fella who will make Anna grand like the *Americano*. I look, and one day at the dogfights there is one fella who fight for me and beat up many men. He is strong and is like a black thundercloud over the mountains in New Mexico. He is the one.

"Making love in the fields is nothing. A man who have a house and will buy high-heel shoes and grand things for Anna is big thing. Because I know I will find him and be no more peon I learn to speak good. I learn to do everything right. And I wait. So now I burn my old dress in the fire. First I tear it in little bits, but that is not enough. So I burn it in the fire. That is so I never put it on again. I will always wear these things that make me very grand, because there are no others. . . ."

The oilstove had burned out. There was a light from the sky, graying the windows. All Melody's tiredness was on him. It was a weight too heavy to bear. He couldn't think. Desire was gone. Sleep was close. He wanted to give in. But Big Mat would be coming in before very long. Without a word to Anna, he got up and tried to pull Chinatown off the cot. Chinatown began to mumble but he was not awake. Leaving him, Melody walked alone to the door. He looked back at Anna and was too tired to tell her much.

"Maybe China tell Mat about the letter," he said.

The fresh air was sour to his nose as he went away.

Big Mat could hear Anna's laugh when he mounted the stoop. Then he heard Chinatown's high voice singing snatches of mill songs. He listened awhile before he opened the door. They were sitting on the floor. With a pair of scissors Chinatown cut at an old newspaper.

"Hallo, straw boss," said Chinatown. He was looking up with a sheepish grin.

"We are playing," said Anna.

"Aw, we jest messin' round," apologized Chinatown.

"He show me how to make dolls," said Anna. "They stretch—so." And she stretched a row of them between her hands.

Chinatown brightened up. "Them's dance-hall gals."

"They dance—so," she said. And she shook her hands. The strip of newspaper dolls danced.

"That little one in the middle look kinda good," said Chinatown. "Man, she got a mean wiggle!"

Big Mat grunted, "Git somethin' to eat on the table."

She crumbled the strip of dolls in her hands and stood up.

"Too much foolin' round here," he said. "Somethin' to eat shoulda been on the table."

Chinatown was accustomed to Big Mat. He knew that his brother did not know how to play. With a foot he dragged a chair within reach. Tilting it against the wall, he sat and watched Anna's broad hips sway in front of the stove.

Big Mat started out of the back door.

Chinatown said, "Melody come with me but he gone now. Brung a letter."

Anna rattled the pots on the stove.

"What sort of letter?" Big Mat stopped.

"Come from Kentucky," said Chinatown. "Reckon Melody took it with him."

Big Mat hesitated. Then he started for the outhouse.

"It don't make no difference," he called. "I ain't readin' no letters from Kentucky no more."

Anna rattled the pots again. There was a clink of glass from the outhouse.

"Big Mat hittin' the booze early," commented Chinatown.

She did not answer. With a spoon she stirred the leftover beans. A side of bacon was on the table. She left the beans and began to slice the bacon. Every movement was studied. She knew Chinatown's eyes were on her.

"Sure is a crime to take you outa circulation," said Chinatown.

Anna smiled. She glanced toward the back door.

"There is a dogfight tonight," she said. "You are going?"

"Dunno."

"Melody is going maybe?"

"Dunno."

"He is funny."

"Who?"

"Melody. He cannot play Mexican tune."

"Maybe I see you and Mat at the fights tonight," said Chinatown.

"I will not be there."

"How come?"

"Mat, he don't let me out. We don't go no place."

"Mat jest ain't the kind to have no fun." Chinatown laughed.

"All my fine clothes stay at home." She sighed.

There was a rustling under the house. Rats played under the floor. Chinatown picked up his rifle and sighted down the barrel. He clicked his tongue when he had drawn a bead on the sound.

"Maybe you will come here tonight," she said casually. "Big Mat will be at the mill."

"What's that?" said Chinatown with a start.

"Oh, you will bring Melody," she said. "He will bring the guitar. There will be corn whisky for you."

"Boy, I can't git no straight on you," puzzled Chinatown. "Jest last night you don't want no part of Melody."

"That is a lie," said Anna.

"It ain't no lie," he argued.

Suddenly Anna was very angry. "I say it is a lie."

Chinatown backed down. "What you so heated up about? Maybe I got things all wrong, but you don't have to git all heated up."

She was sulky. "What the hell it matter to you?"

"It ain't nothin' to me," said Chinatown. Then he added under his breath, "Dunno how come I leave folks pick on me."

Anna swept the beans off the stove. The pot tilted and spilled onto the floor. She swore and got down on her knees to wipe up the mess.

A crunching sounded on the front stoop. She looked up quickly. Chinatown had already opened the door. It was Sugar Mama, bareheaded, a little afraid to come in. Her oiled moon face gleamed.

"Mama!" yelled Chinatown.

"Ha, the one who laughs!"

"I been plannin' to git by your place." Chinatown slapped her on the hip.

"Sure, sure. You come by tonight."

He chanted: " 'Gonna wait till payday to swing down the lane, 'cause nothin' good is give away.' " He thought he heard the outhouse door creaking. Without knowing why, he became nervous.

"See you later on, Mama," he said quickly. "Got somethin' to do now."

Anna rose and wiped her knees on the dish towel.

"What you want?" she asked coldly.

The question caught Sugar Mama in the middle of a grin. The grin twisted.

"Ah, my little one," she cried, "you are wearing such fine things that old Mama think you are *Americano*."

Anna tried to move behind the table.

"What you want?"

"Maybe I just stop for a look at my little one—my sister's own child. But she is so grand now that Sugar Mama does not know if she should come in or go away."

She looked down at Anna's bare feet. Anna had taken off the high-heeled shoes. They hurt her feet. Sugar Mama looked at Anna's dress. The dance-hall dress was like a rag. Anna had it pinned like a diaper between her legs.

"Go away!" cried Anna. "You are an old bitch."

"Yes," said Sugar Mama, "I will go away. It is not right that the old bitch talk with *Americano*—the fine lady who is friends with the fine people who live up on the hills and ride in motorcars."

"Get out!" screamed Anna.

"But yes, I am going to the dogfights in the evening. Of course, you will not go to the dogfights. Tell your fine friends on the hill that Sugar Mama is at the dogfights and let them laugh. Tell them that when next the foreman's wife invite you to eat."

Anna screamed a curse and ran at Sugar Mama. Chinatown grabbed her and held her arms. She kicked with her bare feet at Sugar Mama.

The back door banged open. Big Mat strode into the room. His face was purple black. Sugar Mama gave him one frightened look and turned to run down the stoop. In two bounds he was close enough to help her on her way. His foot caught her in the back. She tumbled into the road, sliding a little in the dust.

Chinatown was afraid that Big Mat was going to jump on Sugar Mama. But he and Anna were pushed back into the house. Big Mat slammed the front door. The frame shack rattled.

Sugar Mama stood in front of the stoop and screamed awful Mexican curses. Her voice carried like a mill whistle. A crowd gathered and began to laugh at her. She picked up pieces of dirt and began to throw them at the house. Then they could hear the voice fading in the direction of Mex Town.

Big Mat and Chinatown were at table. Chinatown wanted to talk about what had happened but he did not dare to break the silence. After they had eaten Big Mat and Chinatown left the house. Anna did not see them. She was busy putting on the high-heel shoes and unpinning the dance-hall dress.

It was evening before Big Mat had drunk all he could hold, yet his step was certain. Chinatown had not drunk half as much but already was beginning to stumble. Big Mat supported Chinatown as they mounted the flat stone in front of the lunch car.

"Got to eat," Chinatown was saying. "You got to eat, too, Mat."

Big Mat was not talking.

"Be sick if we don't eat," complained Chinatown.

They were inside the doorway. Shoulder to shoulder, they blocked the narrow car. A couple of men had to flatten themselves against the counter in order to squeeze out. Nobody paid them any attention. A steel worker who smelled of liquor had special privilege.

Smothers was sitting opposite the coal stove at the far end of the counter. A thick cup shook in his hand. The cup made a steady clatter when he tried to hold it against the saucer. The wild look on Smothers' face was more pronounced than ever before. The other men had left an empty seat on either side of him. He mumbled to himself.

"There Smothers!" cried Chinatown. He started

toward the little cripple. Chinatown was too drunk to notice Smothers' condition.

Smothers started as Chinatown and Big Mat dropped onto the stools on either side of him.

"Steel goin' to git ol' Dusty." His lips were loose.

Chinatown said, "Got to git a bellyful of black coffee. Be too sick to see the dogfights. You got to eat, too, Mat."

"Steel goin' to git Dusty," repeated Smothers.

Chinatown looked at him. "Steel ain't gittin' nobody."

"Steel goin' to git everybody that's leavin'," cried Smothers.

Before Chinatown could give a heated answer a slow voice behind him took up the words: "Sure, steel get everybody. . . ."

There was a man behind the stove. It was Zanski, the old Slav that worked with them in the pit.

Smothers was excited. "See—it's true—steel git 'em all. . . ." He quieted. The cup began to rattle again.

Zanski made a sign to Chinatown. He touched his forehead meaningfully and indicated Smothers.

"Worse tonight. Every month it is worse. They take him away soon. It is better so."

"What he talkin' 'bout?" asked Chinatown.

"It is talk around mill," said Zanski. "Lots of colored fella leave job. They go to big mill near Pittsburgh. More pay for same job."

"Why didn't I hear 'bout this?" fumed Chinatown.

Zanski looked hard at Chinatown before he spoke. "You would not want to go. They get more pay for job because trouble comin'." He leaned back behind the stove.

Clucking at her gum, the waitress drew Chinatown's coffee from the big urn.

"One midnight coffee comin'."

She slid it down the counter. It stopped in front of him. Not a drop spilled.

"Man, that there's service!" Chinatown grinned.

"She is my granddaughter, Rosie," said the old man behind the stove. He got up and took Smothers by the arm. "Come, it is time for job."

Smothers was looking at the mill stacks through the lunch-wagon windows. The smoke from them looked to be liquid, so heavily it rolled.

"Like big guns jest shot off," said Smothers. "Maybe they is guns jest shot off."

"Come, we go," said Zanski.

Quietly Smothers put on his cap, and they left.

A young man at the other end of the counter laughed.

"Ain't never seen Smothers so bad off as he was this evenin'."

An old man looked out of the window at the smoke stacks.

"He ain't so wrong. Mill stacks do a fella in same as a gun. Long time I see kids get white as kids can get and still know what the sun is like."

Three cups of coffee had completely sobered Chinatown. When he left the lunch wagon he was in high spirits, ready for the dogfights.

He tried to persuade Big Mat to come along. "You can't git in more 'n a coupla hours' sleep, anyway, Mat. Might as well stay up. We be jest in time to see the first dogs pitted and maybe win a little somethin'." He fastened his hand on Big Mat's arm.

Big Mat broke away from the detaining hand. He gave no sign at Chinatown's call.

All day he had been drinking green whisky. It had not made him drunk. It could not make him forget the feeling of helplessness when his muscles couldn't make things right for himself and Anna.

There was no light in his shack. Big Mat opened the door softly. Anna was not in the room. The quilt on the cot was in a twisted pile. Big Mat passed his hand over the quilt. Then he sat down to wait.

Three days passed before Melody felt like going back to the job. He had not been worried. For five dollars a doctor would write his name on the sick list. He had sat with his guitar and looked at the book propped against the window sill. That book was Big Mat's Bible. Mat had moved out and taken everything but the Bible. It was strange that he had left the Good Book. In all the time Melody had known him there had never a day passed that Mat hadn't studied the word. Seeing Mat's Bible had given the trouble in Melody another twist. But he had not moved it from the sill.

So all those long days he had been twisted inside. And his guitar sang all the empty notes it had. His own music, he felt, was driving him crazy. Without trying, he had built a song around a tan-skinned girl, the shadow of her legs making a pattern on the floor as she turned down the kerosene lamp.

Dusty-butt Jones and some of the other men had been packing for their journey to the new mill near Pittsburgh. They had complained about the music.

"Sound like somebody dead in here."

"Whyn't you play somethin' happy like 'fore we go?"

"Be glad to go. That music been goin' since day before yestiddy."

"Git drunk an' sleep it off."

"Aw, go to hell!" Melody told them.

Yet he was tired of his own noise after three days. He was tired of it but he couldn't help wanting to play. For the first time he thought it was a bad thing to have to play only the music inside him. He began to wish that his right hand were smashed so never again would he be able to hold a pick.

On the morning of the fourth day he went to the superintendent's office. He had decided to ask for a transfer. The superintendent was a busy man; the interview was short and to the point.

Melody said, "I wants to git off the hearth."

He had not expected to be transferred immediately. He had merely expected the superintendent to keep the request in mind. But Melody was lucky. A man was needed at the blast furnaces. The superintendent gave him a slip of paper to pass on to the boss of number-six stoves.

The superintendent said, "He's colored fellow too. He'll fix you all right."

Melody went straight to the lockers. He wanted to say good-by to his old gang before they left for the pit. They laughed and gave him advice as they struggled into their clothes. He looked around for Zanski.

"The old hunky got his three days ago," one of the men told him.

"Naw!"

"Yeah."

"How it happen?"

"I was up on the hearth. I see when he and Smothers come back from eatin'—that's the last I see. Next thing, O'Casey was bawlin' for a new man. Zanski was gone."

"A dead one?" asked Melody.

"Don't know."

Melody was not satisfied until he had found a man who did know.

"Naw, he ain't dead," said the man, "but he through in the mills. Was just too old to know when to jump. Steel tagged him."

It was good to know that Zanski was still alive. But he was through in the mills. That was something to make a man cry a little. It would be a relief to cry for somebody other than himself. Yet instead of crying Melody smiled. Now the old hunky could sit in his courtyard and watch his kids and his kids' kids go to work in the mills.

The boss of number-six stoves was Bo. Melody remembered Bo's advice that first day at the mills. He started to greet Bo as an old friend. Bo looked at him out of hard eyes and snapped:

"What's your moniker?"

"Melody."

Then Bo looked at his crew. His mind ran: Two micks, a ginny, a hunky and a hayseed. "Boys," he yelled, "this guy is Melody."

Nobody said anything.

"Take a look around," snapped Bo. "See how things go. At noon start in dumpin' cinder."

Number four was not in use. Melody climbed the winding ladder and sat atop the furnace. He had several hours before noontime. He took out his tobacco and rolled a smoke. A little way across the yard was the open hearth. Big Mat would be just getting off. Melody had tried not to think about his reasons for transferring. He wanted to make himself believe that he had just gotten tired of seeing the same old faces every day—doing the same kind of work. But in the back of his mind he knew that all those reasons were linked to a jealous hatred of Big Mat. Unconsciously he had acted to keep that hatred from growing. Now he would not have to see Big Mat go home to Anna.

Just before noontime Bo came up the ladder and

sat with Melody. He thought that Bo was going to
give him hell for not looking around as he had been
told to do. But Bo was sociable.

"Got the makin's?"

"Sure." And Melody passed the sack.

"Lucky for you this blast not workin'."

"How come?"

Bo drew the sack shut with his teeth and talked
while he rolled the cigarette.

"Bad gas always on top the furnace. Kill you
quick as hell. Got to be keerful not to spend no
time top a live furnace, boy."

"Obliged."

"That's all right. I had a eye on you."

"Obliged."

"Sure. How come you wanted to git on a stove
gang?"

"Jest tired o' the hearth, that's all."

"Sure."

They looked across the yard and smoked.

"I'm the only nigger in the mill got micks
workin' under me," said Bo.

Melody gave him a puzzled look.

"That's how come I got to be so short with you
when you come in," said Bo.

"Oh."

"I got to show no favorites and be eight times
as good as the next man."

"Reckon so."

"Somebody all the time gunnin' for me. Don't
like to see a nigger in my job."

"Then how come they to make you a boss in the first place?"

Bo laughed. "Same way all us niggers got here in the first place—'cause o' trouble. If it wasn't for trouble wouldn't be no niggers in the mills at all."

They let that drop. Soon it was time for Bo to go if he wanted to get his eating done.

"Luck with that cinder," he called.

"Obliged."

He was halfway down the iron steps. He turned and threw his voice against his hand.

"Be keerful and don't walk the top o' this furnace. Ain't been rebuilt yet. Bad blowout."

"What kind o' blowout?"

"Slip. Killed a guy. That's how come you to git your new job."

The work at the blast furnace was easy to learn. In three or four hours Melody was working in rhythm with the stove gang. There was very little real hot work. It could not be compared to the open hearth. Working next to the bosh, the base of the blast furnace, was cool in comparison to the hearth when there was a front wall to be made. And the four big stoves, heating the air blown through the blast furnace, were nothing when he remembered the pit below the pourers' shelf.

However, there was plenty of heat for the stove

gang after the furnace had been tapped. They had to push a mud gun right up to the dripping tap hole. The gun shot mud under great pressure. They had to shovel like madmen to keep that gun supplied. It did not take long to seal the furnace, but he was glad the tap hole did not have to be mudded often.

On the last turn of the day Melody smashed his right hand, his "picking" hand.

He had been thinking of the guitar, knowing it could never plunk away the craving that was in him. In the South the music makers had said, "A love cravin' gits so mixed up with the music you can't tell which is which." Melody had said that also. Now he knew it for a fact. The last three days of picking at his guitar had wearied him. Yet he knew he would not be able to let the music box alone.

That was what he had been thinking. Now he was lying with his hand quivering at his side, and blood ran in hot circles around his fingers. He would always wonder if he had done it purposely. That was how it seemed at the time.

They had been working on number four when it happened.

Bo had said, "It ain't no use in them buildin' this here furnace again. Once they blow out like this jest the spot where they was sittin' is jinxed. Everythin' is jinxed."

But the superintendent had kept the men working on the furnace. He laughed at their grumbling and put Bo's gang to cleaning the flue dust out of the gas chambers.

"Somethin' bound to go wrong," Bo had muttered.

Number four was cold, but they had worn wet handkerchiefs over their faces. Even with that protection they had only been able to do minute shifts inside the stoves. The heat stung through the handkerchief when they poked blue dust out of the hivelike chambers.

Melody had entered the stove with Bo. In the lamplight he should have been able to keep out of Bo's way, but his mind was on the guitar. He had put his hand in the wrong place. He had seen Bo's rod come down. It had been like watching something in slow motion. Then had come the shock. There was no pain. Now he wouldn't be able to pick a guitar for a long time.

The next thing he saw was the crowd of men around him. He was down on the floor in front of the water trough. Bo leaned over and spoke to him. He did not answer. He was trying to figure out if he had done this to himself purposely.

Chinatown could see the dark windows of Big Mat's shack when he turned a bend in the dirt road. He began to curse softly. It was coming dusk. If Big Mat had been at home there would be a lamp lit. Perhaps Mat was already at the hospital. He,

too, could have been at the hospital if he had not
given time to this useless trip. He started to turn
back from the dark windows. But the door was
close at hand.

"Hallo!" he cried to the dark room.

There was a shadow on the bed. He waited until
it took form. It looked to be Anna.

"Oh, I almost went off," he said to the still form.
"Thought the place was empty."

There was no answer. He came in quickly, the
lighted lamp choking in his hand. Holding the
lamp in front of him, he advanced slowly.

Anna snapped her eyes open. She blinked in the
light.

The lamp almost dropped.

"Boy, you give me a scare!" he breathed.

She sat up and began to rub her eyes.

"Jest come by to pick up Big Mat." He set the
lamp on the table. "Waited for him at the mill.
Didn't show up."

"Mat—where is Mat?" she mumbled.

"He musta gone on to the hospital—after me
wastin' all this time."

"Mat is gone to the hospital?"

"I reckon so."

"Mat is hurt?"

"Naw. It's Melody." He saw her quick breath.
"Nothin' bad. Smashed a hand, they said."

"Melody smash a hand?"

He looked at her closely. "Say, ain't you awake?"

She drew her hand across her face. He could see

her skin puffed and cloudy with old blood. That old blood made the shape of a hand.

"Mat been at you," he stated.

She went to the dishpan and threw water on her face. Bending, she managed to wipe away the water with the front of her dress. Her lips began to bleed.

Chinatown gave her his bandanna to daub her lips. He saw where they had been cut against her teeth.

"You goin' to the hospital with me," he told her.

"I hold kerosene in my mouth," she told him.

"Naw, them doctors know more 'n you."

There was no will in her.

"C'mon, git in your shoes," snapped Chinatown. "Ain't got all night."

With childlike obedience she knelt and began to fish under the bed for her shoes.

Chinatown watched her bent back. Then his half-ashamed grin widened his lips.

He said, "They fix you up good while I'm seein' Melody."

She felt his sympathy, and response showed in her body.

When they walked out into the road Chinatown held her steady.

"Mat a hard man"—he sighed—"but he ain't mean."

"It is right for the man to beat the woman," she said.

"It jest that Mat don't know how to laugh," he insisted. "He ain't mean."

They walked across town until they came to the trolley line. There was a fifteen-minute wait for a car. In that fifteen minutes Anna bared herself to Chinatown. There was sympathy in him but no understanding. That made it easy for her to talk. She could tell and still keep her secrets.

Three nights ago she had come home late. Mat had been waiting. He had seen the wet of the ground dew on her back. There were twigs in her hair. He had known she came from lying in the hills. He had been wild.

It was true—she had been lying in the hills. But she could not tell him that she had been chilled, miserable and alone there. She could not tell him that she had done that for Sugar Mama's benefit. He would not have believed. Only that morning he had kicked Sugar Mama into the dirt road.

Yet on that morning she had followed China-town and Big Mat when they left the house. Had they glanced behind them, they would have seen her. The dance-hall dress was unpinned from its diaper shape. The high-heel shoes were on her feet. She had kept the two men in sight until they turned off to buy whisky. Her path led straight on to Sugar Mama's shack.

Why had she gone to Sugar Mama's shack? It was simple in feeling but hard to tell in words. She wanted Sugar Mama to think that she was on the way to one of the fine houses back in the hills, because Sugar Mama had taunted her. She wanted to hurl those taunts back at Sugar Mama.

She had not gone into Sugar Mama's house. She yelled the lie from the road. Sugar Mama had come to the porch and laughed and cursed, and she had cursed back. But she knew that the lie had missed its mark. Sugar Mama was not fooled.

Then a puzzling thing had happened. She found herself walking into the hills instead of circling back as she had planned. No, she had not been out of her head. She knew that there were no friends waiting in the fine houses back in the hills. She knew that the intent of her trip had been merely to trick Sugar Mama. But she did not turn back. She had not understood with her mind. . . . Her body was proving something.

So she had crept close to one of the white hill houses. Cars had come up the drive. Afraid, she had hidden herself in the bushes at the foot of the hill. All day she was there. Lying on her back, she had watched the house—almost above her where it hung over the hill. When the moon came out the early dew wet her. Her body had lost strength to the ground. Tired and dispirited, her body could barely take her home.

Big Mat had slapped her around. He had made love to her tired body. It had not responded to either. He had gone to work twice and come home twice. Everything remained the same. Yesterday he had left the house. She did not know where he went. He had not come home.

She was really talking to herself—not to Chinatown.

The trolley came. They took seats at the rear of the car, and Anna had to stop talking. The passengers kept craning to look at her bruised face. She pulled her shawl together, hiding her head.

Bo had come to the hospital with Melody. He felt responsible for the accident. But there were no bones broken. The doctors had joked while they cleaned the wounded hand. They laughed at Bo's worried face. He'd have to hit harder next time if he wanted to cripple a steel man. Melody would be reporting for work within a week.

Melody carried the bandaged hand in his coat pocket when they left the hospital. He had felt the hurt when the broken flesh came to life after the first numbness of the blow. Now there was no pain. In a detached manner he noted his heartbeat by the dull pulse throb of the hand.

He counted to himself. "One, two, three . . ."

"You all right, boy," stated Bo. "Ain't hollered once."

Melody counted by threes. "One, two, three— one, two, three . . ."

"Yessir, you all right. Hear your brother's all right too."

"Yeah, yeah, yeah," he muttered, with the beats to mark the count.

"Wonder why they ain't been near the hospital?"

No answer.

"You ain't split up or nothin'?" ventured Bo.

Melody stopped counting. He thought a second. "Maybe we kinda split up."

"That's too bad," said Bo. Then he added: "I hear good talk 'bout the one call Big Mat."

"What you hear?"

"Hear he one of the best helpers they got on the hearth."

"That's a fact."

"Hear the micks calls him Black Irish too."

"Yeah. That's all you hear?"

Bo fussed with a pipe. He started to speak and changed his mind. Finally he said:

"Well, I did hear he took hisself a woman."

"Yeah."

"Lots of guys do that," he said defensively.

"But he got a wife in Kentucky," Melody burst out. "He got a wife to send for. She there waitin'."

Bo got the pipe lit. He puffed slowly to collect his thoughts.

"So that what you split up over," he mused. "Well, I figure you more worried 'bout that than him, huh?"

"I reckon." Melody felt guilty, because he had not told the whole truth.

"Could see somethin' was eatin' at you this mornin'."

"Things ain't right!" he cried.

"Things ain't right nor wrong, boy. Things jest is."

"Things is all messed up."

"Look, boy." Bo knocked his pipe against his palm to give emphasis. "Most ever' nigger in this mill got womenfolks back where they come from. Still, most ever' one of these niggers is hitched one way or another to women round here. They don't bother 'bout no laws or nothin'. They jest ups and starts out a new way. I don't know why it is, but it ain't nothin' to upset a man."

Bo was practically a stranger to Melody. It suddenly was embarrassing to be talked to like that by a near stranger. Melody felt as though he should say something formal to put them back where they belonged.

"Much obliged," he said. It was all that came in his mind.

Bo was apologizing when he muttered: "I had me a wife once—ten children back in Dixie. Now I got me a little bitch round here. So I figure I kin talk."

Not looking at each other, they watched the dark road beneath their feet. A couple of blocks away they could hear the roar of a trolley. The roar died as the trolley stopped near the hospital. They kept their eyes on the road. They had no reason to be curious.

All of the stove gang were at the lunch wagon when Melody and Bo walked in. A man who had been hurt on the job was a particular kind of hero to the men who had worked beside him. Just that morning Melody had met with silence when Bo introduced him from the blast-furnace floor. Now the crew hailed him.

"Work back in easy, kid. Work back in easy," said the Irishmen.

"How your hand do for himself?" asked the Slav.

"You stand pain like anything," said the Italian. "I tell fella on night crew that you Italian. I say you gone back to Italy."

The hayseed just took Melody's hand and parted his freckles in a grin.

Bo left Melody with the gang. Before he went he said: "Don't worry 'bout your job on the blast. I git your brother, Chinatown, in your place till you git back. He'll start the long shift in the morning."

Melody took a cup of coffee and sat back near the stove. He had to learn to hold the thick cup steady with his left hand. So he practiced, sipping at the heavy coffee. Listlessly he half listened to the gang's kidding of the waitress.

The girl popped her gum and matched them word for word. She drew a cup of coffee and leaned over the counter. In her own tongue she spoke to someone behind the stove.

The answering voice rang old chords in Melody's ears. He saw a hand hook out for the cup. He knew that hand. Many a time it had been hooked over his own to lift a slag hunk from the pit floor.

The gang was kidding again.

"Who you got back there, baby?"

"Your sweetie, heh?"

"The boss ain't gonna like that, baby."

Melody leaned backward to look. The old Slav sucked his coffee in the shadows back of the stove. He saw Melody. His head nodded up and down. His eyes crinkled. Melody started back to where he sat.

The waitress was back at the coffee urn. Her voice crackled.

"Don't be so Goddamn funny. It's my grand-father."

The kidding stopped.

Melody sat on a box in front of Zanski. He nodded at Melody again.

"Yes, yes—my big girl, Rosie—a fine girl born at mill but like girl in Ukraine."

"Yeah," he agreed. "She do all right back o' the counter too."

The old man stroked the long, uneven beard away from his lips and took another sip of the coffee. His faded blue eyes became thoughtful.

"No, no," he said, "she is not like girl in Ukraine. Don't look for husband and have kids. Girl around mill work in box factory, eh? Make food in lunch-room, eh? Get money like man."

Melody didn't care what the old man talked about. Zanski was a good guy to be with. He liked the sound of the talk, but, like all talk nowadays, it came from a distance. Wound up in his own world, he half listened, half dreamed.

"Man don't tell kid nothin' at mill," the old man was saying. "Not Rosie. Rosie don't listen to old guy with bad arm, eh?" He tried to move his left arm to point up what he was talking about. That arm was held across his chest by two big safety pins. "Fellas tell you I get tagged. Now I don't never go back to mill." He smiled. "Goddamn steel do a good job—take skin off arm—fix chest up like fella peel onion. No work no more . . . So, so, so . . ." he chanted.

Zanski leaned back in the chair to suck at his coffee.

Without volition Melody's right hand fingered for the tobacco sack. The bandaged hand fumbled out through the coat pocket.

"Sonsofbitches!" he gasped, and he brought the quivering fingers to his mouth. But he could not suck through the bandage.

"You got hurt hand, Melody?" asked the old man.

"Jest mashed up a little."

"You don't say nothin' much. How it happen? Hot metal ain't burn?"

"The hell with it!" he told him.

"You don't be mad. Laugh at me just like you. Old man try to take bath in hot metal, eh?"

"I ain't mad," he said.

"You got problem, eh?"

"Naw."

"Somethin' up here." He taps his forehead.

"Look," he told him, "there ain't nothin' wrong up here. There ain't nothin' wrong nowheres."

"So?"

"So?" He mocked the broken English.

The old man went into a shell. His eyes took on an untroubled, vacant look. He sucked at his coffee.

Melody had not meant to hurt the old man. He waited for him to loosen. He waited, but the eyes kept in the distance.

"I jest ain't myself today," he finally ventured.

"So?"

"Been off my feed a long time," he said.

"So?"

"Yeah."

Zanski was still in his shell. Melody was forced to give in all of the way. "I reckon you hit the test square in the middle. I kinda all balled up here." And he tapped his head.

"You nice fella, Melody," said the old man. "We get mad quick like boy, eh?"

"Yeah," he said, and grinned at him.

"Sure, sure. We get coffee—forget him."

He leaned out from behind the stove and beckoned to his granddaughter. She came, popping her gum.

"Why the hell don't you go home?" she said to him. "All day you sit around here. The boss 'll chase us both out."

The old man beamed on his granddaughter. He

reached out his good hand and took hold of her skirt. He pulled her close to the chair.

"Rosie, Rosie," he said, "what I tell you?"

"Aw, all right." She took the gum out of her mouth.

"This my frien' from mill," said the old man, nodding at Melody. "This is Rosie. Shake hand."

The girl put her gum behind her ear and then shook the hand.

"Pleased t'meetcha," she said.

"Didn't know you and him was kin."

"Sure."

"Bring one cup coffee for my frien'," the old hunky told her.

The girl told him, "Whyn't you go home and get coffee? All the time you hangin' around here. The Goddamn coffee is for sale."

"So . . ." The old man gave her a little push.

She started back for the counter. She went a few steps and turned.

"Midnight?"

"Yeah." Melody nodded.

"Comin' up."

The old man leaned back in his chair and loudly honked his nose into a bandanna. He spoke through the handkerchief.

"Old fella, long time dead now, tell story in my village. Story all about man get devil in his head. Scare him out with big shout. Now I tell my kids if they get devil in head come talk quick. Devil grow if fella don't say somethin'." He blew his nose and scrubbed at his mustache again. "You and me don't tie bandanna round neck no more." He chuckled. "Just wipe nose, eh?"

"That's what they made for," Melody said.

"You get a little coffee. Feel good. Maybe you talk out devil, eh?"

Before Melody could think what to say Zanski leaned from behind the stove and cried:

"Rosie, why you so slow?"

In a few seconds Rosie brought the coffee. Melody sipped at it and tried to think how to get around telling the old hunky all that was on his mind. He wouldn't want anybody to know about Anna—about that night in Big Mat's shack.

The front door slammed open, and a wave of fresh air went around the stove. Chinatown had just come in. Melody knew his loud voice.

"China!" he called.

Chinatown came at a run.

"Melody! Melody! You got to come quick! They got Mat."

"Who got Mat?"

"The sheriff down near Pittsburgh. Say Mat was tryin' to kill a fella."

"Tryin' to kill what fella?"

"They ain't say in the telegram."

"What was they fightin' for?"

"Ain't say that either."

"What for you waste time?" asked Zanski. "Brother in trouble, eh?"

"What kin I do about it?" said Melody.

Chinatown looked as though he had been slapped in the face.

"Ain't you comin'? Ain't you——?" he stuttered.

"What kin I do?"

"You mean, you ain't comin'?"

"Naw."

Chinatown couldn't understand. As though to familiarize himself with all the facts, he checked on his fingers:

"First, Anna and me come to the hospital. But you jest gone. So I go by the bunkhouse. You ain't there. But there the telegram on your bunk. I wait at the bunkhouse. I wait at Anna's. I don't know what to do."

"Where Anna now?"

"They kep' her at the hospital," said Chinatown. "Her lips was all cut up."

Melody leaned forward and shocked himself with the fierceness of his own voice.

"Look, China, Big Mat a man, ain't he? He know what he doin'. If he try to kill a fella and get caught at it, then that jest his hard luck. He don't need me to look out for him."

"I don't know what you talkin' about," cried Chinatown desperately. "What we goin' to do?"

Melody was like another person seeing himself, a stranger to himself. A drum in his head throbbed desperately.

"You go on back to the bunkhouse and sit on your ass—that's what to do."

And suddenly he couldn't bear for Chinatown

to be there looking at him. In a fight two men had stood breast to breast, and then one of them got that fear in his eyes when he knew he had to die from the hog sticker pushing into his belly. He knew it and he didn't know it. Melody couldn't bear Chinatown to look at him with that fear in his eyes. He hopped off the box and gave Chinatown a push. Chinatown fell against the stove.

"I don't know what's the matter," he stuttered.

"Git outa here! Git!" Melody yelled at him.

He backed out of the way of the stove and, keeping his slant, scared eyes on Melody, backed out of the lunchroom.

The men of the stove gang were all on their feet, looking, saying nothing. One by one they paid their checks and filed out.

The old hunky said, "Wait!"

A lot of cuss words started up from Melody's belly.

"For drink coffee," said the old hunky. "Boss throw Rosie out for waste coffee. You drink, eh?"

"Can't!" he snapped. "Got some business."

"You go git brother?" said the old man.

"Naw, he kin rot," Melody cried.

"Where you go?"

"Same as I told you. Got to see a fella 'bout some business."

But he started out to do what he had known he must do. It would be a long trip to that place near Pittsburgh. He would have to start right away if Big Mat was to be free by morning.

Zanski watched him go. Rosie came and stood by the chair.

"Colored fella ain't have woman keep white curtains in a man's house. No kids. Fella ain't got kids move no place. He stop at grave." He leaned back and patted one of her broad hips. "Pretty soon Rosie get married, eh? I move some more quick."

Chinatown should have been feeling good that morning. The world had swung back to a familiar pattern. Melody was on his way to get Big Mat out of the jailhouse. He was going to hold down a job at the blast furnaces until Melody was ready to take over. It was like old times—the Moss boys working like a family should work. But there was something wrong that morning. The wrong was not in him—it was in the air about him.

Smothers hobbled at his heels on the way to the mills. He didn't say why he wanted Chinatown's company. Neither of them had anything to say. Both men marked the strangeness of that. They were two whose mouths had always been full of talk.

Once or twice, from the corners of his slant eyes, Chinatown caught Smothers' face. It was a face full of random movement. The corners of the lips were hard and soft in turn; the eyes were big, to show white around the balls, looking inward; the thin nose flared wide at its base, searching the wind.

But Chinatown was glad for Smothers to keep shut. There was his own self to search. He was walking along, feeling like a spring coiled on a hair trigger. He didn't exactly know—his body just felt as if something were going to happen. His body was getting ready for something.

Only once before could he remember feeling like that. A long time ago, down in Kentucky. To get away from what looked like a cottonmouth snake he had dived through a thick bush. He had not known what was on the other side. It seemed a year to think in while he was sailing through that bush. But his mind couldn't tell him anything. It was his body that had talked, had warned him that he was going to land hard. And, sure enough, he had landed in a trap of broken slate. He had broken a leg that time.

Now his body was flashing that same warning, telling him that he was going to land hard.

An icy shiver passed through him when Smothers spoke.

"Keep a sharp lookout! Look sharp, ever'body!"

"How come? How come?" he asked, but he knew.

"I got grief in my bones."

Smothers was in dead earnest. The quake in his voice sent another shiver through Chinatown.

A distance from the mills all sounds softened into one another; up close every sound had its own history. Through the roar of the Bessemers the ear-splitting cries from the plate mills began with a whine and ended in a strangled rasp. Engines panted and struggled with the rails. The ore boats along the river kept up their own noises. Each tin house had its own pulse. And above everything an organ of whistles sighed and bellowed.

These things had not come to be commonplace to Chinatown. The mills would never be his home. His gold tooth was still a token, keeping his mind south of the Mason-Dixon line.

They checked in together. On all sides men were headed for their jobs—not running but, to Chinatown's eyes, making great speed. He had that same feeling of haste when he started for the blast furnaces. To him life in the mills was stepped up. Inside he ran more slowly.

When he passed the open hearth he kept his eyes open for old friends. He could see one of the gangs working like crazy men to draw the heat before turning the furnaces over to the new crew. Now and again, through openings underneath the hearth, he glimpsed the pit men, swinging to get the last cleanup over and done with. A man called out to him from a tin shack. The voice sounded high and off key. But things were just different that morning. He was hearing and seeing in fine detail, as a man does in the awareness of danger.

Smothers had separated himself from Chinatown but now he came hobbling back. He pointed toward the blast furnaces.

"Trouble," was what he said.

A little knot of men stood in the yard around one

of the blast furnaces. They were hand-rolling cigarettes and chewing cut plug as though this were
quitting time instead of the starting hour for the
long shift.

Chinatown saw Bo at the water trough. He
trotted toward him. Smothers swung along on his
sticks.

"What the hell!" hollered Chinatown. "You
guys ain't gittin' ready?"

"How many is dead ones?" panted Smothers.

Bo did not glance up. He bit off some rope tobacco. He spoke through the juice when they were
close enough for him not to have to raise his voice.

"They jest got a special crew. Tryin' to git that
Goddamn number four ready."

One of the Irishmen in Bo's gang came toward
them.

"This here rest don't make me mad." He
grinned.

"Startin' in is always bad," said the other Irishman. "I can do a shift one handed after I get heated
up."

"This here number four a jinx," growled Bo. "I
tell you it's a jinx. Yesterday Melody gits hurt.
They work all night on it, and now the water
cooler burn out. No sooner they git that fixed than
the damn thing begin to freeze up. Look like for a
while she's goin' up. Took a lots of guys off the
other crews. Put everybody behind."

Another of the gang heard what was being said—
the Italian stove tender.

"Sure as my name John—sure as pope—sure as anything—furnace gotta devil in him."

"It don't do no good to jest line and half ass fix around a cold blast," argued Bo. "I tell you that a long time ago."

"You sure said so." The hayseed nodded.

Smothers had been trying to get in a word, but the men didn't want to hear his raving. They kept shifting to keep him from latching onto a group. Finally he stopped and cast his eye around to catch every man within hearing distance.

"Ever'body better be on the lookout. Steel liable to git somebody today. I got a deep feelin' in my bones."

Bo hollered, "Maybe steel gonna git you, Smothers."

Smothers was glad of someone to take notice. He hobbled up to Bo.

"It gonna git somebody. I know it's got to git somebody."

Bo laughed. "Well, if it's you, Smothers, we make you up into watch fobs. The boys round the bunkhouse 'll wear you across their vests for luck."

Chinatown knew what Smothers was feeling. His body was flashing that same warning right along.

He said, "You say yourself there a jinx, Bo. Could be, 'cause I been feelin' somethin' ever since I started out this mornin'."

John, the stove tender, crossed himself and muttered in his own tongue.

One of the Irishmen laughed. "You ain't super-
stitious, eh, John?"

"Not me," said John. "I ain't believe nothin'."

"Then what was you sayin' to yourself?"

"Oh, that ain't nothin'." John grinned. "Just old
prayer. Lotsa times fella wrong. Better be on safe
side."

Smothers broke in, "There ain't no safe side."

The Irishmen laughed.

Smothers grabbed Chinatown by the arm.

"You ain't a bad guy, Chinatown. You know old
Smothers talkin' sense."

"Sure, sure." Chinatown tried to pull away.

"Ever'body laugh when I tell 'em what I know,"
said Smothers.

Chinatown was embarrassed. He pulled away.

"They jest laugh 'cause they scared, I bet." And
he laughed.

Smothers grabbed again. He caught the hayseed.
The man shoved his shirt back into his pants.

"I know steel and ever'thin' talk to you," he said,
"but it's tellin' you wrong when it tells you to tear
up my clothes."

Smothers clawed at him.

"Somebody got to believe me. Steel gonna git
somebody."

"Shut up, you crazy fool!" hollered the hayseed.
The freckles grew dead white against his flushed
face. He whirled on the other men. "Whyn't somebody make this Goddamned nut keep quiet?"

He barely managed to duck from the path of the

stick Smothers swung at him. The men laughed. For an instant the hayseed wavered between anger and the laughter of the men. Then he grinned. Before Smothers could move the hayseed had snatched both of his sticks. Laughing, he held the sticks up for everyone to see.

Smothers started forward. But his legs could not hold up. Spitting curses, he fell to the ground. That made the young hayseed almost split with laughing. Then he stopped his noise. With an innocent gesture he made as though to stop the game. He held the sticks out to the crippled man. Smothers grabbed. The sticks were again drawn out of reach.

That kept up—Smothers dragging himself over the ground toward the sticks, every few feet falling forward on his elbows when he tried to grab.

The men were laughing.

Chinatown recalled Smothers' strange dignity. He did not like to see him in the dirt.

"Sure is a shame to plague a cripple that-a-way," he said to Bo.

"Heard somethin' today," said Bo.

"Aw, make them cut it out!" insisted Chinatown.

"Fella was tellin' me 'bout what happen to a gold tooth in the war."

"Somebody ought to stop it."

"Fella said that after a fight some guys would go over the stiffs with pliers and pull all the gold out'n their heads."

"Damn!" said Chinatown.

"Yeah," said Bo. "Got so the colored boys would pull out their gold ones and throw them away. Ascared of bein' shot in the back."

"Damn!"

Bo's eyes wandered to Smothers.

"If I said anything they think I stickin' up for Smothers jest 'cause he's colored."

"Glad I wasn't in the war," breathed Chinatown.

Bo said, "Naw, I can't mix in. Only one in the mill with micks under him."

The hayseed had gotten tired of pestering. He tossed the sticks into the water trough. Cursing, Smothers began a slow journey toward the trough.

One Irishman said, "Maybe that'll learn that Smothers not to be a wild man."

The words spurred Smothers. In a convulsion of movement he reached his goal and got his sticks under his armpits. Then he turned toward the men, and his voice went into a scream.

"None of you fellas knows why you's runnin' wild when before you come here you was tame. Ain't none of you got no idea. But I know."

A few men came out of the furnace house to see what was going on. They stood grinning with the rest. The Irishmen laughed outright.

"Listen, and I tell you so you'll know somethin'," screamed Smothers. "I tell you 'bout a fella who been around here a long time. Once he's one of the best catchers they ever put on a roll table. But that's once upon a time. Now he ain't nothin' but a old cripple-leg timekeeper. The boss men

jest job him around 'cause they kind of sorry for
him. Don't think he don't know that.

"He work a farm down in Texas for a hell of a
time before he ever see a rollin' mill. Then he don't
really know how he ever got in this here valley.
It's jest that one day he find hisself the best catcher
along the river. There plenty of frogskins in his
pocket, and them greenbacks buy more corn
whisky than he kin drink. He kin sleep with women
that he git lynched for jest lookin' at back in Texas.
So what he do then? He go crazy. He try to make
all the money, screw all the gals and drink all the
corn whisky in the valley. And one day that same
corn tell him he's big as God A-mighty. It's the
heat of the steel makin' that corn boil inside him,
and he vow to walk the roll tables from one end of
the mill to the other. And half the rollers bet he kin,
and half bet he can't. There's two thousand dollars
say he will and he won't.

"Them roll tables takin' steel full speed, and his
corn whisky walks him halfway down the line and
leaves him there on his own."

No man was laughing now. They all leaned forward. With this madman they were walking half
the length of a big roll table, dodging white-hot
steel shuttling full speed across and between the
crushing rollers. Men forgot to spit their tobacco,
and spit-rolled smokes burned right down to
cracked lips.

Smothers was still talking. "I said his corn

whisky leave him there, and he ain't able to go on under his own steam. The heat saps him all of a sudden, and his legs give out. Some fellas run to shut off the power, but he's crawlin' on his hands and knees, tryin' like hell to git over the side of that table. He almost make it, too—woulda made it if the fella who was s'posed to stop the table hadn't got fussed and, instead of stoppin' the table, reversed it —reversed it and sent a hot bar 'cross that table-walker's legs."

One of the listeners started a soft chant that was like little explosions in among Smothers' words.

"Goddamn . . . Goddamn . . . Goddamn . . . " went the chant.

"There wasn't no pain," screamed Smothers. "There wasn't nothin' but the steel all over the mill, yellin' an' laughin' fit to kill. Roll steel git him . . . roll steel git him. . . . Yellin' an' laughin'."

Smothers' voice went up into a song. "It was *me* the roll steel git! It was *me!*" Then the high voice slid down the scale to its regular whine, and misery dropped over his face. And that made it as though those steel voices were still yelling and laughing in his ears: *Roll steel git him . . . roll steel git him. . . .*

"All the time in the hospital I kin hear that steel talkin'," said Smothers. "I kin hear that steel laughin' an' talkin' till it fit to bust my head clean open. But I git well. Steel didn't git me that time like it think. I come on back to the mill on two sticks.

They give me a job where I can set down most of the time. But, settin' or standin', I kin hear when cold steel whisper all the time and hot roll steel scream like hell. *It's a sin to melt up the ground,* is what steel say. *It's a sin.* Steel bound to git ever'-body 'cause o' that sin. They say I crazy, but mills gone crazy 'cause men bringin' trainloads of ground in here and meltin' it up.

"So when I git so I kin hear what steel is sayin' I know jest why I go wild and git drunk and try to walk the roll table. I know why all you guys runnin' wild and goin' crazy of a Monday. It's that crazy-mad steel whisperin' and yellin' all the time, makin' men crazy-mad too."

The men did not say anything. When they went in to work they were still silent. Hours passed before anyone had a word for the shamed hayseed.

The Italian crossed himself again and was not questioned.

That night, when a break came in the long shift, Chinatown walked out of the blast house. He saw the pointed stars of fire along the edge of the Monongahela. He looked up in the sky at the points of fire so much like those along the river. He took his last look at all of these. And he remembered Smothers' words to the green men: "Somethin' dropped right out the sky, blazin' down, lightin' up this old river in the dead of night." A warning out of the sky. That was strange—iron dropping out of the sky. Maybe it was a sin to melt up the ground. He didn't know. He felt now as he had felt before—lost and full of great changing fears that he didn't understand.

The points of fire along the river marked an endless line ahead of the old Ford. Melody was at the wheel, his bandaged hand resting across the spokes. Big Mat was at his side. It hadn't been hard to arrange Big Mat's release: a six-hour trip to the place where he was being held, a payment of twenty-five dollars for his having disturbed the peace. It might have gone harder with him, but the man he had tried to kill had not pressed the charges.

Big Mat and Melody had not much to say between them. And now they were nearing home. It was a cool, clear night. The wind from the river blew around their heads. They were not a. brothers, but the river wind had blown away all the hot passions in them.

When they reached the first familiar section of the river front they were ready for talk.

Mat muttered, "I kill anybody I catches creepin'."

Melody gave him a quick look. He had thought Mat a victim of corn whisky and a drunken brawl. He had not even asked the name of the man Mat had tried to kill. He wanted the talk to go on but was afraid to say Anna's name.

So he said, "That there's what you say back in Kentucky."

"I say that and I means it," Mat grunted.

"Who the man?"

"Dusty-butt Jones."

"You mean old Dusty?"

"Followed him all the way," he grunted.

"What he do?"

Big Mat shut up and turned his collar against the wind.

Melody cursed himself. He should have waited for Big Mat to bring it out naturally. He knew his brother. Mat would go into a shell now.

But he was wrong. When the car rolled into town Mat turned to him.

"Stop here a little."

Melody pulled up in one of the little dirt roads. He made a cigarette, using one hand and his teeth. Slowly he lighted up. The river front was like Christmas time. On Christmas night, back in the red hills, the men had formed a square and tossed lighted kerosene-soaked balls of waste. For the eyes of their women sitting high on the hills they wove a fire pattern. Fire balls were being thrown now when he shifted his vision through the faulty windshield. These remembrances of the past, together with the distance of the mills, gave him a strange detachment. He sank back.

Big Mat said, "Melody, you and me ought not to be dodgin' each other."

"Naw."

"I been thinkin' my head goin' to break open if I don't talk to you."

"Maybe I ain't the guy you ought to talk to."

"Ain't nobody on God's earth I ever talk to 'sides you. And I got to talk what's in me."

"Maybe I ain't the guy."

"Sometimes I think I goin' to go wild and kill off some people that ain't done me a harm," groaned Big Mat.

"You ought to talk to somebody 'sides me," insisted Melody.

"I know you think I ain't actin' right 'bout Hattie," he said, "but that ain't all on my mind."

Melody wanted to know about the man Mat had tried to kill. But something made him insist.

"It's jest that I ain't the guy to talk to. It ain't jest Hattie neither."

"There ain't no use in thinkin' 'bout old things," Mat said. "I stop studyin' the word. It ain't no use in thinkin' 'bout preachin' the word no more. But that ain't all on my mind right now."

Melody looked at him with old eyes. He looked like a man who had just lost a fight. And Big Mat had never looked that way before. Many times he had been slapped and kicked around. But always before he had had a resentment in him that kept him still a man. Now he was a paper sack, full of nothing—like an empty paper sack. He looked as though he were too empty for anything ever to fill him again.

Melody said, "Lots o' guys round here jest starts out on a new way. It ain't nothin' to upset a man."

He did not know he was repeating what Bo had said.

"It got so that little gal, Anna, mean somethin' big to me. I reckon I must look kinda like her paw. I ain't so young. . . ."

"It ain't nothin' to upset a man."

"She a woman, jest the same," he said.

"Yeah."

"At first everythin' go fine. At first she hold onto me like a woman hold onto her man. Now——"

"She ain't tried to run off?" Melody could not keep the jump out of his voice.

"Naw, she don't run off. Leastways, her body don't run off. But, jest the same, she ain't there no more. I don't know how come, but she ain't there no more."

"How you mean, Mat?"

"I don't know how I mean. Ever since that night she come in late. She wouldn't talk. She wouldn't even tell me a lie. I beat her up some. Her body was around. But she jest ain't there."

"What you mean, Mat? What you mean?"

"I don't know what. In bed she jest lay there and don't say nothin' and don't do nothin'. She do what I say do, but it seem like bein' on top a piece of ice. She a long way away all the time—jest like I doin' somethin' to a dead body. But I do it. And then I feels bad. So I starts in hittin' her. And I feels badder. It make me crazy."

Melody felt a strange, high sensation. And he relived the hot room and Anna fighting with him for a letter. He felt filled with running feet, feet running in all directions. His eyelids beat like moth wings.

Big Mat said harshly, "I think she lettin' some fella creep when I gone to the mill. That got to be it. Somebody creepin' when I'm gone."

Melody snapped into cold anger.

"The bastard you tried to kill," he stated.

"That what Sugar Mama told me. She told me she seen Anna pass her place and Dusty-butt with her. She told me she seen him creepin' round my back door. Sugar Mama tell me all that, so I foller him clean down the river. Woulda killed him if the law hadn't got me. But Sugar Mama lied."

"Sugar Mama lied," repeated Melody.

"Dunno why, but she lied. He ain't the man. He give proof he ain't the man. But still I try to kill him."

"How come?"

"Dunno how come. Jest seem like that had to be it. Seem like things was all right if he was the man."

Melody nodded. Now it seemed all right for Big Mat to try to kill a man who had done nothing. Maybe he was getting kind of crazy himself.

"Maybe you kin tell me somethin', Melody. Maybe you kin tell me."

There was nothing. Inside, Melody could have repeated those words for himself. He needed to tell himself what it was all about. He couldn't talk. He could put out his hand and touch Mat.

"Tell me somethin'!" cried Big Mat.

He gripped the bandaged hand with a force that paralyzed Melody's right side. Melody was whirled to face him. Looking into the lined face, Melody felt weak.

"All right—all right—it be all right," he stammered.

For a hundred years Mat stared at him. Then he relaxed his grip. He had shrunk a little.

Suddenly Melody was aware of the warning. He started up. There was great danger. Something screamed it inside him. His head rang with the fearful shrilling. He thought the mill whistles were blowing. Something was going to happen down by the river. He knew it. His whole being was gripped by that knowledge. He had no memory of anything that had gone on. Big Mat, Anna, himself as himself did not exist. Only danger was real. A steel man would understand. That warning did not tell of death. He had seen men die: furnace gas, electric shock, falls into the pit, slides of piled iron on the narrow-gauge railways—all that was expected. No warning had come for them. This warning was for something much worse. Perhaps the monster had gotten tired of an occasional victim. Perhaps he was about to break his chains. He would destroy masses of men, flesh, bones and blood, leaving only names to bury. Fear of that drove everything else out of a man.

"Mat! Mat!" he cried.

Big Mat raised his head and sniffed at the air. It was deep night. The river front was a lighted string. He rose to his feet and stood beside Melody. They held onto the windshield of the car. They watched the string of light.

Then down there came a blinding flash. Straight up into the sky it went, shooting its reflection to the far shore of the Monongahela. For a moment the windshield of the car filled with light. A mushroom cloud, streaked with whirling red fire, followed the flash. Under its giant bulk the blast furnaces stood like black pop bottles. Then the sound boomed over the car in a big wind. The windshield rattled.

They were stunned.

It was over that quickly. Perhaps it hadn't happened at all; perhaps their senses had played tricks. But the smoke mushroom hung in the sky and lay along the water.

One of the black pop bottles had foamed over down there at the edge of the river.

Melody started up the automobile, and they headed for the mills. It was slow going through the town. Every person able to walk was headed the same way. There was no rush. None of the women were hysterical. The kids kept quiet. The entire town just moved on the mills. The streets were full of swinging lanterns.

People were held in the car lights now and again, like motion-picture slides: Slavs—women with shawls over their heads—Mexicans whose hair shot back grease glints, a couple of black girls, wearing old carpet slippers, men, big chested, with handlebar mustaches, people with sweat misting on their faces, black faces, tan faces, red faces. . . .

The crowd was already thick in front of the mill gates. Uniformed guards were stationed there to keep anybody from slipping through. They knocked men and women back. Some of the men began to grumble.

Big Mat and Melody wormed through to the gate and tried to get one of the guards to look at their work cards. They were knocked back with the others.

"Just wait! Just wait!" the guards bawled.

So there was nothing to do but stand and wait. Exactly what there was to wait for nobody knew. And yet there were no questions.

A light rain began to fall. It was chilly. Most of them had not stopped to put on coats. With an excited clanging two ambulances drove up, their headlights parting the crown. The gates swung open, and the white automobiles slid through. And now a whisper began to pass among people.

Melody heard it: "Number four on the blast went up. . . ."

Melody's gang had been at the blast furnaces. Some of them might be dead ones. Chinatown had been working in his place. He might be just a cinder now. But some of the tension went out of Melody, because he knew what had happened.

He gave the whisper to Big Mat. And he could hear it travel to the outskirts of the crowd.

A different look came over the faces. Men lit cigarettes, and the women, beginning to feel the chill, huddled closer together.

After a while there came another whisper. "Fourteen are dead ones . . . fourteen. . . ."

They passed that whisper along without emotion. The people grieved behind set faces.

When the ambulances came back through the gates there was a sickening smell of burned flesh. Even the hard-faced guards had to turn away for a minute. In that minute Melody had slipped through the gate and was racing toward the blast furnaces.

There was a shocking silence around the blast houses. Billowing steam rose slowly from the broken furnace that had been number four. A lot of men were standing around looking, doing nothing. He caught one man by the shoulder.

"Who was the dead ones?"

He was not answered.

He asked everybody he saw that same question. Nobody would answer. Then he saw Bo sitting over to one side. There was a group of men around him. He was not hurt.

"Bo! Bo!"

For a long minute he looked with blind eyes. Then he said, "Hallo, Melody."

"Where's Chinatown?"

Bo looked back toward the furnaces.

"Like a bottle of bad vinegar," he said. "Foamed over jest like vinegar."

"Where's China?" Melody shouted in his ear.

One of the men answered for him.

"Don't ask him nothin'. He ain't ready to talk."

"My brother was in his crew," Melody said.

"Musta been taken away," said the man.

Five

FOURTEEN MEN GONE, and Smothers one of them. Fourteen men, and of Bo's crew only himself and Chinatown alive. This was a sorrowful time. There was no need for mourners; there were plenty. The entire town mourned the death of the fourteen. It was a time of funerals throughout the town. The Italians buried their dead after feasting; the Slavs sat like rocks and watched their flesh go to the earth; the Negroes were full of loud wailing and made a three-day wake for their sacrifice.

Smothers had spoken the truth at last. Then he died. The steel workers understood the way of the accident. A shelf of hot metal had built itself high up in the faulty furnace. When that shelf had broken the force of its fall had been explosive. The upward rush of the blast had blown off the entire top of the furnace. Tons of stock had been thrown into the air. That was why fourteen men had had to die. But steel workers also felt the truth of Smothers' last words: steel just had to get somebody that day. There was no conflict between what Smothers had said and the facts. None of the experts who came to the scene of the accident could tell why a slip had come to number four.

It might have been better if the list of dead had run to fifteen. Chinatown's eyes were gone. It was as if Chinatown were gone. For the man who had had those grinning, slant eyes it was one and the same. The day that they took away the bandages even the doctors' tempered minds were struck with horror. For Big Mat there was only a dull, dry misery, but tears rolled on Melody's face as he looked into the dead things that were no longer eyes. They were old eggs rotting in their ragged half shells, purple and revolting.

The doctors said that those once-eyes would die and shrivel through the years, that then they would look better. Now it would be better to hide them under black patches.

Weeks had to pass before Chinatown knew his blindness. That long time he was a man thrown into a vacuum. He did not know where he was; he did not know where the light had gone. There was no time. In movement his body felt motionless; the floor was a thing that moved to touch his feet. This was not delirium. He had been a man who lived through outward symbols. Now those symbols were gone, and he was lost.

Big Mat and Melody had taken a bigger house so

Chinatown could be near to them in his trouble. Anna took good care of his body, but it was Melody who saved his mind. In his first groping for some familiar ground he slipped back into the past. Melody went with him.

"Man, man!" Chinatown said. "Chitterlin's and cabbage greens!"

"Got to have some fat meat," said Melody.

"Maw out in the back-door garden gettin' them greens."

"Gonna git some fat meat too," said Melody.

"Gonna git that tooth," he said.

"Which tooth, boy?"

"Gold one."

"Man, it sure do shine!"

"Got to keep that tooth." Chinatown struggled upright. "I ain't nothin' if I loses it."

Melody remembered the boxcar and the long, dark trip.

"Sure, boy. Whoa, boy!"

Chinatown strained into the darkness. He leaned his body far to one side as he fought the curve.

"Ascared to sleep . . . ascared to sleep. . . . Car shake so it liable to knock the tooth right outen my head. Now I sleep, and maybe it git knocked out. . . ."

"I keep talkin', boy. . . . I keep talkin'. . . ." sang Melody.

Chinatown stopped. He whispered, "You heard what happen to young Charley?"

"They lynch him," said Melody.

"Yeah, they lynch him in broad daylight," cried Chinatown.

"That's a long time ago," whispered Melody.

"That's a long time ago?"

"Sure, that's a long time ago."

"Gonna wrap me a smoke," said Chinatown. His hands fumbled with the air.

Melody rolled a cigarette in one hand and stuck it into the tragic mouth. He put a match to one end, and Chinatown drew breath. The weed burned fiercely.

"This don't taste like no tobacco," cried Chinatown. He spit the cigarette. Melody picked it from the bed and crushed the fire between two fingers. The burn felt good to him.

"Smoke spoil my feelin' for eatin'," cried Chinatown. "Wish I had me a smoke."

"Ain't no tobacco around," said Melody.

"How come you don't play somethin' on your box?" he asked.

"Sure, boy." And Melody reached for his guitar.

"Blues drive away that hungry cravin'," said Chinatown. "I jest sit here in the warmth and listen."

Melody's hand was out of the bandage, but he couldn't make any music. The corns were gone from his picking hand. He couldn't get tone from the strings without those corns. It was all off key. He couldn't feel the music. Sitting with Chinatown and looking into those rotted eyes had made him feel sick. Chinatown had laughed at the woman whose left breast had died and rotted so no man would buy her for a dime. Their Maw had told them when they were little scapers in the red hills, "Never laugh at a hunchback, or you'll carry his pack." Chinatown's eyes looked so rotted that they brought back to Melody the memory of the woman on the road. Always before Melody had been able to heave and then feel clean. Now he could not let his stomach turn because of his brother's eyes. They were with Melody to stay. He would never be able to spew them away.

Chinatown began to feel for the present.

"Ho, Melody, what was that 'bout the mills? What was that what Smothers said? All the time my body jumpin' like hell. I don't like it . . . I don't like it. . . . Mill never be my home. Who keep them circus animals down by the river? Melody . . . Melody, gimme a glass. I got to see my tooth. Only it's too dark. What good a gold tooth in the dark?"

Melody could not stand this. He went away in an old song.

"China," he half sang, "you know where I wish I was at now?"

This was the wishing game, a part of their past, forgotten up to now. Chinatown had always liked the wishing game. He hunched forward on the cot.

"Where at?" He grinned eagerly.

"Me—me," pondered Melody, "me—I wish I was long gone at noontime. That's it, long gone at noontime. . . ."

"Where you be goin'?"

"Be jest long gone, that's all. Treadin' the ground, walkin' the whole earth wherever there good ground and somethin' growing."

"Maybe you plant a little molasses cane?" China-town ventured.

"Maybe later, but I can't stop now. I got to cover the earth 'fore midnight—got to feel all the good muck ground with my toes."

"Seem like you stop jest to suck jest one little cane joint, then——"

"That's right," said Melody. "I stop jest to cut one. But I suck it, treadin' along. The muck feel good to my toes, and there always the swamp near by to blow cool on me."

"Maybe you step on a cottonmouth in the swamp. What you do then?"

Melody thought a little and let his thought ride high through the endless spaces of his mind. He hit a bad chord on his music box. But it was good enough to carry him on a bit.

"I do meet up with a snake," he cried. "A whole land full of snakes come at me. First there come a coachwhip. He grab a root in his mouth and lash at me with his tail. But he don't last long. I stomp his head deep in the ground. And he spring up into a tall whitewood tree. Lash the air a little at the tip so the leaves 'gin to fall."

"You meet any more snake?"

"I'm ridin' high till I meets a hoop snake, rollin' along, rollin' along, with his tail gripped in his jaws.

Boy, what a snake! Solid round like a wagon wheel. He gain on me. I'm treadin' the air, but he ridin' the breeze. Then I curve on him till he rollin' round and round, scarfin' the ground, rollin' himself down. So when I push his head in the ground there ain't nothin' left but a crooked wild chinaberry tree, curved in the wind and broken like a old wagon wheel."

"Man!" breathed Chinatown. "Tell me 'bout the rattler."

"Ain't much to tell," said Melody. "He a tree full of jack-o'-lanterns now, rattling when the wind blow."

"Aw, that one wasn't nothin'," complained Chinatown.

"Maybe he a tree full of sunned acorns," said Melody. "Then he rattle like dry bones at drought."

"Where the blue racer?"

"He so pretty I wind him round my neck in a bow tie."

"Where the barn snake?"

"He a string of red and yellow beads for the neck o' a gal."

"Where the snake look like a root?"

"He a walkin' stick, like a branch o' juniper."

"Where the spreadin' adder?"

"When I come up on him he unjoint himself. Ain't nothin' but a lot of little pieces underfoot. All I got to do is mix him around with one toe. When he come back together there his tail at the wrong end, his head in the middle."

"What you do when midnight come?"

"Come midnight . . . come midnight . . . well, I go look at all the farmers. They all black. There ain't no white man in the land. Nobody gits crop-aliened. There ain't no ridin' boss. The muck ground cover all the farmers so they grow potatoes under their armpits. They grow field corn between their toes. One man jest let a big tree grow on his back for shade. All he do is walk in the shade and drink corn whisky."

"Don't he drink nothin' else?" asks Chinatown.

But Melody has no chance to go on with the game. Chinatown has traveled in the past and now he wants something out of the past.

"Melody," he said, "I sure would like me some of that red pop. Git me some of that red pop."

"Sure, boy," said Melody. "I git it right now."

Melody was glad to leave the wishing game unended, glad to leave the house for the red pop. Anna took his place with Chinatown. She could not quiet him until she took one of his hands and drew it within the bosom of her dress. Melody saw. He looked into the corner where Big Mat crouched. Big Mat had closed his eyes.

Every telephone pole, every fence carried a placard. In big black letters the steel workers were urged to come to the union headquarters and sign up. "Union Meeting Tonight," advised leaflets

strewn in the road. Melody saw these. But his eyes
did not carry the message to his brain. To him
everything had disappeared with Chinatown's eyes.
He did not resent the mills because of what they
had done to his brother. Somehow or other it
seemed now as though he had known all along that
it must happen.

The explosion had helped the cause of the union.
The Slavs and Italians were joining in large blocks.
When Melody walked up to the lunch car there
was much talk passing between these men—talk
that died when he entered. He knew many of these
men but he was black. As yet nobody knew where
black men stood with respect to the union. They
called his name but kept a suspicious eye on him.
It was not well to talk too openly. A stool pigeon
could bring a union man to grief at the job. When
he had gotten his red pop and gone the talk would
flare openly again.

Melody was not anxious to get home quickly.
He needed relief from Chinatown's eyes. He took
the long way. Anna would take good care of Chinatown. Like all her kind, she had a ready sympathy
for a maimed animal, whether dog or man. He
thought of her easily now. Since the night of the
explosion she had occupied only the rind of his
mind. All the deep parts of him were taken by
Chinatown. He had the gift of a sympathy so complete that his brother's eyes became his eyes.

There was a funeral air in the bunkhouse. Bo
was there. He sat on the floor in the middle of an

intent audience. No one spoke. Their attention was for Bo and for what he did. Between his legs was a pile of little steel scraps. In front of him burned a tin of canned heat. Bo put a steel dish on the heat. Into the dish went a few pieces of lead. Then he sat back to wait.

Almost hypnotized by the strange air, Melody sat on the floor to wait.

For twenty minutes they sat. Nothing sounded but the sudden scrape of a boot against the grain of the floor. Then the massed breathing of the men began to grow until it whistled. A watch in someone's pocket ticked louder and louder. The creak of the bunkhouse in the changing air came now and again. Each man heard his own heart circling its blood. So what was silence spoke louder and louder.

Then the time was up. The lead cupped the bottom of the dish, a heavy dust scumming its brightness. With ceremony Bo broke that scum. Then out of his pocket came the little chains. A drop of lead fastened each chain to one of the steel scraps. Shortly he was through. Bo began to pass out these newly created watch fobs. Afterward the group broke up.

Melody went along home, the gift in his pocket. He had not needed to ask questions. He knew of Bo's strange promise to Smothers that day of the explosion. That promise had been in a joke, but the joke had turned on itself. ". . . if it's you, Smothers, we make you up into watch fobs. The boys round the bunkhouse 'll wear you across their vests for luck. . . ."

One Sunday, when Melody dressed in a regular suit, he would wear that little piece of Smothers across his vest for luck.

Everything was the same when Melody got home. Only Big Mat had gone. He had gone to walk in the hills, Anna told him. Melody was glad. Big Mat was no help, crouching always in a corner of the room.

"Well, had to go clean to hell and back, but I got it," he told Chinatown, waving the red pop.

Chinatown tried to find the pop. Melody took his hand and closed it over the neck of the bottle.

"It don't feel right," said Chinatown. He bit off the cap. When he turned up the bottle it spilled down both his cheeks. He tasted the first mouthful only. "Ugh! I knew it." He gagged. "This don't taste right neither. It ain't red pop." He spat out the stuff.

Melody did not know what was the matter.

"That there's red pop," he insisted.

But Chinatown could not taste the color red.

Big Mat was caught in emptiness. The trouble with Anna had broken his confidence. Chinatown's mishap had struck its blow, so Mat had been split like a bag of wind between two heavy palms. But he was not unhappy in the house with his brothers and Anna. His brokenness was his adjustment. The fact that Anna would not sleep with him was hard on his body, a big body which made constant demands. But he had held himself in before. He did again now.

He took to walking in the hills. Like his brothers, symbolically he was going home. In his trouble his spirit was near home. So the song of the mills was muted, and all that he saw had another air. The sky sometimes took on the colors of planting time. He did not see the smoke and slag of the mills. There was that coming-summer smell that the hot gases could not kill. This time of the year did something to Big Mat, and he found himself away in the hills, digging in the ground now and then with a pointed stick. He walked, and his nostrils widened in the light wind. His nostrils tested the wind for the smells. There had been an old mule pressed against a rail fence on a sloping red hillside. Its nose had felt the breeze for good smells.

"This smell like a good year for things in the ground," he would mutter.

He would be far away from the river, up in the black hills. Because he listened for other sounds he would lose the sound of the steel makers.

"Would be long planted now iffen we was back home," he would tell himself.

These would be good days. Sun behind the thin gray clouds, the earth trim under his shoes. These would be good days for sick men to feel the earth.

"Long planted now," he would repeat.

Sometimes Melody would be with him. China-town was more able and no longer needed a string to tie him in the world. He could be left with Anna for longer and longer periods. On these occasions Big Mat felt older. His body had begun to reflect his mind. It became evident. When Melody climbed the steepest hills Big Mat chose the path around. Often Melody would have to stop and wait for his big companion. When they lay down to gain breath Melody would be the first up for a new climb. In the evenings, when they left the mills, Melody's quick flesh would throw off its weariness; Big Mat's fatigue would hang on. Once Big Mat stopped by the roadside and picked up a great rock. All that long walk he kept it balanced in one palm. Melody did not speak. He could not have lifted the stone.

But July was coming on, and with it came the end of the Moss boys' retreat to the past. With the coming of July, it was difficult to walk through the town. The attitude of the foreign workers was changing. Big Mat and Melody found out what that change could mean. It was early Saturday, on their week end away from the job. They were approach-ing the pump at the edge of town. As usual, there were the Slav women with their pails, waiting in line for washing water. A ball game went on in the cleared space behind the pump shed. Suddenly one of the boys spied them.

"Ya-a-a . . ."

The stones began to whiz in the air around their heads. A stone caught Big Mat on the chest. It sounded a deep note and fell at his feet. He stood bewildered. Melody was not bewildered. This all had a familiar air. There were the women pulling their shawls down over their faces. Those faces held deep contempt. Big Mat wanted to stay and talk, but Melody pulled him away.

"What the trouble?" Big Mat kept crying.

But Melody did not answer. They cut through one of the side streets. There were faces in the doorways. Every second he expected to see an old Slav with a long handle-bar mustache lean out of a window to spit at them. There was no old Slav this time, but the workmen lolling in the doorways gave them long, level looks. Those looks were more terrifying than threats.

Big Mat had been known as Black Irish. That title had meant something to steel men. They had known of Big Mat before they had met him. And after the meeting they looked with respect. The Slavs had accepted the judgment of the Irish. Big Mat could not understand this sudden reversal.

At the end of the dirt road the houses stopped. Beyond were the hills. They quickened their pace. A man came slowly down the street. It was Zanski. Big Mat was relieved. Zanski was their friend. All would be explained. Greetings on their lips, they waited. And Zanski passed them as though they did not exist. Melody called:

"Hey, Zanski! Look!"

"It's Melody and me!" cried Big Mat.

Zanski was undecided. Then he turned and walked up to them. They put out their hands, and Zanski took them. But they were all suddenly self-conscious.

"See your arm out of the sling," remarked Melody.

"Yeah. Three, four day now," said Zanski.

"How Rosie gettin' on?" asked Melody.

"So . . . so . . ."

"Chinatown gittin' better. Gittin' around," spoke up Big Mat.

"That's good."

"Ain't been able to git no more corns on my pickin' hand," said Melody, wiggling his fingers.

"So . . . so . . ."

Big Mat started to speak, but Melody cut him off.

"Well, we be seein' you. Got to git walkin'."

Zanski waited for a second.

"All my boys is join the union," he stated.

"Yeah, yeah," said Melody.

"Well, so long," they said to him again.

As they walked on Zanski called:

"Do not go around the corner. There is trouble."

They did not know what he meant. Melody turned and waved.

"So long."

"What got in ever'body?" asked Big Mat. "You know he seen us in the first place."

Melody did not get to answer. They were rounding the corner. They saw an almost motionless scene: a group of men bunched over a man who was lying in the middle of the road. There was no action to indicate a struggle. It was more like a group of young men gathered to look at a sick man. They started forward.

"Somebody fell out maybe," said Melody.

Then a strange thing happened. Like a fan unfolding, the men fled in all directions. In a moment there was no one on the road but the two Moss boys and the sprawled figure.

Melody and Big Mat wanted to see what danger would present itself. They did not approach. A lean hound with staring ribs came out of a hole in a garbage pile. He was full of rotten food but he trotted up to the fallen man and smelled around. He gave short whines, and the concave of his stomach jerked as though it were full of rubber bands. He opened his mouth. The sounds of his coughing broke as he continually reate his gorge.

Melody picked up a rock and threw.

"Scat, you!" cried Big Mat.

Melody threw again and caught the hound in the side.

With a short yelp the dog fled in a tight circle. It was not the stone—he was trying to escape the sudden pain of madness, running away from the thing in him that whirled him like a top. At last he set a straight line for his flight. Over the prone body, across the piles of garbage, until he was gone in the hills. His faint, crazy yelps hung in the air.

Big Mat and Melody walked with cautious steps up to the silent figure. They remembered from their boyhood—these were dog days, hot July up into August, when snakes shed their winter skins and dogs and men went mad.

The man on the ground was Bo. He had been kicked and beaten. There was a lump the size of a pigeon's egg at the base of his skull. They knelt beside him, chafing his hands and rubbing his stomach.

"Gotta git some water," said Big Mat.

He lifted the unconscious man in his arms. The weight was nothing. He started at a fast walk toward the pump. Melody walked along by his side, holding onto one of Bo's dangling hands. Both of them kept their eyes moving from side to side. They were frightened deep inside. That fear did not stem altogether from what had happened. It had roots in mob-fearing generations of fore-bears in the South.

The women left the pump when they came into sight. The Slav children kept at a distance and watched them with their burden. They laid Bo on the damp boards beneath the spigot. Big Mat pumped, and Melody held Bo's head to one side so that the water would not choke his breathing. Bo began to stir.

"What's the matter? What's the matter?" And he fought the water, clawing with his hands.

Melody held his hands.

"They gone, Bo. They gone."

With a rush Bo came to himself. He sat up, eyes flaring.

"They caught me," he cried. "But that's all right. I know who they was—I know."

Big Mat and Melody were closer than Bo to the South. They did not question. The first thing to do with a black man in trouble was to hide him. Without heeding Bo's protest, Big Mat threw him, sacklike, over one shoulder and started for home. They had cut across a vacant lot and gone through several alleys before he listened to Bo's words.

"Put me down. I kin make it, I tell you."

Bo was set on his feet. He stood for a minute rubbing the lump on the back of his head. Then he felt his ribs.

"How you feel?" asked Melody.

"Sore as hell, but ain't nothin' broken," said Bo.

"Didn't know you was gittin' it," said Big Mat. "How come you didn't yell some?"

"Didn't have no chance. They hit me too quick."

"Was they tryin' to kill you?" asked Melody.

"They wish I was dead 'fore I git through," said Bo. "I know who they was."

"Who was they?" asked Melody.

"They the bastards got turned off the job 'cause they workin' in the union," said Bo. "I know 'em, ever' one."

"How come they jump you?"

"Say I'm the stool pigeon that told on 'em."

"Damn! How come anybody think you do somethin' like that?"

Bo's eyes became very crafty.

"C'mon," he said. "Let's git on. Ain't no tellin' if they followin' us."

Big Mat turned into the wind. The muscles in his arms twitched.

"This here the North," he said. "We kin fight back."

"Naw, c'mon," said Bo.

They followed him toward the river.

"Whyn't you go by the hospital and git checked over?" said Melody.

"I got business at the mill," said Bo. "I appreciate it if you fellas walk that way with me."

"Sure, sure."

On the way to the mills they passed a few Slav and Italian workmen who looked at them with hard eyes. Once they passed a couple of Irishmen. The Irishmen called to Big Mat:

"Hello, Black Irish."

Big Mat waved his hand.

"Them Irish got sense," said Bo. "They ain't gittin' mixed up with no union."

"How come?" asked Big Mat.

"They all got good payin' jobs," said Bo.

"What the hunkies want with the union then?"

"They lyin' to 'em. Say they kin git rid of the long shift. Eight-hour day what they want. Want more money, too, and a union for all the time. Lot of other stuff."

"Sound all right," said Melody.

Bo looked at him.

"That ain't no way to talk."

"How come?"

"Well, you a nigger. Only reason a nigger in the mill is cause o' trouble. I tell you that before. Only reason I git my job as foreman is 'cause I stick when the rest strike."

"Maybe I git to be a foreman this time," said Melody.

"Maybe," said Bo.

Big Mat was not thinking about the labor trouble. Yet he knew that he would not join the union. For a man who had so lately worked from dawn to dark in the fields twelve hours and the long shift were not killing. For a man who had ended each year in debt any wage at all was a wonderful thing. For a man who had known no personal liberties even the iron hand of the mills was an advancement. In his own way he thought these things. As yet he could not see beyond them.

There were a lot of uniformed guards at the mill gates. They stopped Bo short.

"You got business, buddy?"

Bo looked at the two Moss boys, then he went

up to the guard and whispered close to his ear. The guard changed his tone.

"Okay, I'll call him up. Wait a minute."

Bo stood back with Melody while the guard went into the stone hut by the gate. They could see him working the telephone. Then he kicked the door with his foot and was out of sight.

Big Mat and Melody looked out of the corners of their eyes at Bo. Bo shifted a little under their sidewise glances. He began to talk in a casual way. But they could not keep the suspicion out of their attitudes.

In a second the guard was back.

"Okay, go on in." He gestured to Bo. "He's waitin' for you in the office."

Bo left them.

They stood a few minutes. They had never heard of a steel worker having business in the offices at off hours. The same suspicion hit them both: maybe Bo was a stool pigeon.

"Beat it. Ain't nobody allowed to hang around," said the guard.

They walked slowly away.

They were topping a little rise when the string of railroad cars came down the river front. There was something familiar about this train. They could not quite place the feeling. Then Melody knew.

"Say, Mat," he said. "I know. Them boxcars is filled with men."

Mat looked.

"They ain't full of freight," he said. "Don't see no consignment tags."

"They full of men," flatly stated Melody.

"Niggers?"

"Guess so. Ain't no need to bring white men in that-a-way."

"Yeah."

They stood on the little knoll and watched the boxcar maneuver through the maze of tracks along the river front. They could tell which rails the toy-like engine would choose. The right of way gleamed brighter than the less-used tracks. The train made its way up these brighter tracks. And, by some strange parallel, their minds also chose brighter tracks. Through the things under their vision they sensed the relationship of themselves to the trouble in the mills. They knew all of those men herded in the black cars. For a minute they were those men—bewildered and afraid in the dark, coming from hate into a new kind of hate.

Then the brighter tracks of their minds faded, and what they felt was lost. The fact that both of them had experienced a similar feeling was not strange. Always there had been a harmony between them. They continued homeward. They had been too long away from Chinatown.

But the train came to a stop. It discharged its black cargo. Tomorrow the tension in the town would be heightened. Here was another trainload, an afternoon load. The morning load was already settled in a specially built bunkhouse. And the

Negroes were grouped sullenly around the leaders of the moment. They were here for four dollars a day and a chance to fight with white men. They did not care what the issue.

Through August and into September things were different on the job. Melody and Big Mat knew hardly anyone now. They could not tell exactly who was missing from the job. It was just that every now and then the thought would come: "There's one I never saw before." That new face would be disturbing, because it had taken the place of one so familiar that it had ceased to exist. Those new men did not respect hot metal. The clang of the ambulances became a daily sound.

"Watchin' these guys scares me," confessed Melody one day.

"How come?" asked Big Mat.

"Makes me see how near death I was when I first come round here."

But steel had to be made. No matter how many men were hurt, the furnaces must be kept going. A furnace that lost its fire was like a dead thing. It had to be torn down to the ground and built anew. That cost money. So the new men, like the new men before them, worked, and some of them died. But the flow of steel did not stop.

Somehow it seemed to the men from the red hills that the idea of flesh-and-blood striking was a crazy thing. The fire and flow of metal seemed an eternal act which had grown beyond men's control. It was not to be compared with crops that one man nursed to growth and ate at his own table. The nearness of a farmer to his farm was easily understood. But no man was close to steel. It was shipped across endless tracks to all the world. On the consignment slips were Chicago, Los Angeles, New York, rails for South America, tin for Africa, tool steel for Europe. This hard metal held up the new world. Some were shortsighted and thought they understood. Steel is born in the flames and sent out to live and grow old. It comes back to the flames and has a new birth. But no one man could calculate its beginning or end. It was old as the earth. It would end when the earth ended. It seemed deathless.

But men were going to strike against steel and the way it was made. That was sure to be. The talk of stool pigeons and the discharging of union men did not stop the meetings of the steel men. The threats of the police and the arrest and fining of union organizers did not stop the threat against steel. Steel would not bend, and the men who made steel became as hard as that metal. Yes, there was going to be a strike.

The union organizers made a desperate effort to induce the black men to join the movement toward a strike. But the steel interests had bought the black leaders. Big Mat and Melody found that out through Bo. Bo had brought two Negro politicians to speak to their own. These politicians both said the same thing. A victory for the mill owners would be a victory for the Negro worker. The black worker, they said, had never advanced through unions. He had only advanced fighting alongside of the owners. "Do not forget," they said, "that the men who now ask for your help in a strike are the men who have spit at you on the streets because of your color." Melody and Big Mat had been deeply impressed by that talk from black men who used big words. They said as much to Bo. Bo was contemptuous.

"Them bastards use big words but they don't know much as me. And I ain't paid off for what I say."

"You mean, they git paid for talkin'?"

"Sure, they paid off. Maybe they talkin' facts, but it's all the same to them. They tell a lie for the same money."

Melody and Big Mat could not believe it.

"I know," said Bo. "I work in with the office myself but I ain't paid."

Melody hung on Bo's words. An old suspicion became a certainty.

"Then you did git them guys fired," he accused.

Bo was on the defensive.

"Maybe them guys was fired 'cause I said I seen 'em goin' in the union place. But hell! I got to keep my job. I got to do what they say. Don't forget

I'm the only nigger in the mill got micks under him."

That was true. Bo was a big man in the mill. Melody did not want Bo against him. If Bo was able to get white men put off the job he could even more easily do the same to black men. Melody became afraid. He pulled Big Mat away, for fear of what might be said.

"How come you pull me?"

"This kinda got me all mixed up."

"I don't like no stool pigeons," grunted Big Mat.

"But we on their side, looks like."

"I ain't on no stool pigeon's side."

"But you ain't with the union."

"Naw, I guess I ain't."

Melody thought a second. The puzzle brought lines to his forehead.

"Bo stoolin'," he mused. "Lots of these hunkies who gittin' fired is all-right guys. Now them talkers gittin' paid off." He made a weak movement with his hand. "I reckon us best git along home an' stay there."

Those were good words to Big Mat.

"Yeah," he agreed, "the more I hears 'bout this here mess the less I know."

Big Mat and Melody were vastly different men. But both of them approached the world alike. Ideas of union and nonunion could only confuse them until that time when their own personal experience would give them the feeling necessary for understanding.

So they went home and did not listen to any more talk. There were other meetings and other speakers, both for and against the union, but the Moss boys stayed by themselves. They kept away from the bunkhouse and its arguments. On the job there was whispered talk between spells, but they kept their ears closed against it. They no longer stopped at the lunch wagon. There was no good greeting for them at that place. They did not even walk in the town—the town was hostile to the point of danger.

More than anything else, Big Mat spent his time watching Anna. Every little movement of her turned in his eye. He caught the slant of her big hips as she rested on one stiff leg and stirred in the cooking pots. He marked the way she sat, with her hands dangling loosely between her knees. He watched her comb her hair and bite her heavy underlip as the comb tore through the tangles. He watched her washing her face. Her body bent forward over the pan, her buttocks curved out over spread, arched thighs. He looked through the back door and saw her leave the house, the crinkled, gaudy dress clinging to her body as she walked.

When Melody was not with Chinatown he was sitting close by Big Mat. He felt easier of mind when he was near his big brother. Melody was sensitive enough to feel the pain in Big Mat's loins. And because of that Melody was drawn to him. Big Mat was full of pain for Anna. He, too, was full of pain for Anna. But Big Mat was now focused on something that he might, if he chose, take in his hands. Melody was full of emotions that fell and rose like clouds rolling in a still evening sky. Who could get his hands on a cloud? So Melody sat with him and felt with and through him and tried to get Big Mat's simpler meanings to hitch onto the clouds.

Those heavy clouds rolled in Melody and one day they woke him from his daytime sleep. Both he and Big Mat had been working the night shift. But he knew that Big Mat would not be abed. He doused his head in cold water and went into the kitchen. There was Big Mat sitting in his corner. There was Anna standing in front of the stove. There was Chinatown cleaning his rifle, his blind eyes following the work in mock sight. Melody took the guitar for the first time in a long while. He wanted to do no more than sit cross-legged on the floor near Big Mat. He wanted to hit soft chords that nobody would hear. But all he did was to feel where the corns should have been on his picking hand.

The front and back doors were open, and a good breeze came through the house. The wind pressed at Anna's skirt. It did not disturb her heavy oiled hair. A bit of straw caught in an updraft and settled on her face. She slapped at it absently. She smiled to herself.

Melody could see one end of that smile. It displeased him. There was much trouble in this house. There was much trouble at the mills. What did Anna find to smile over? He watched her face. She had a bright look. Her eyes had been dull. Now they lay in her face like two bright toys. She looked as if she knew a secret. She had an air of biding her time.

Chinatown began to fidget in his chair. He looked about helplessly.

"What's the matter?" asked Melody.

"I got to go out back." He got up from his chair, using the rifle as a walking stick.

Anna moved to his side.

"Leave him go by hisself," said Big Mat.

Anna looked at Melody.

"He got to learn sometime," said Big Mat.

Melody nodded. Anna moved away.

"I can't find it," wailed Chinatown.

"Feel round the wall," said Melody.

With a terrified look Chinatown felt his way along the wall. At last he found the door. Backward, he made the step to the ground. Through the doorway they watched him. For a few steps he showed confidence. Then his foot rolled slightly on a stone. He was thrown slightly off balance. He did not regain that balance. Stepping very high, like a man about to climb a hill, he staggered about the yard. Every few seconds he would sway around, feeling for the familiar touch of the outhouse. He began to cry.

Anna could not endure it. She ran out into the yard and put his arm across her shoulders. Together they went into the outhouse.

Big Mat and Melody stood in the doorway.

Anna reappeared. She led Chinatown back to the stoop. He was still disorganized. He began to talk wildly about the rats he had heard the night before. They might come on him, he thought, and he would not be able to sight his rifle. Anna tried to reassure him, but he would not listen. He had begun to think that every night noise was made by the big rats.

Anna said, "They are not rats. They are sparrows makin' nest for the night."

"They was rats," he cried. "You don't know, 'cause you ain't been round at night."

Anna looked up quickly, fear in her eyes. But Big Mat had not caught the words. To quiet Chinatown she took his hand and drew it into the bosom of her dress.

Big Mat watched the bulge made by Chinatown's hand. His eyes were red from want of sleep and a little mad. He choked over his feelings, trying to find the words to match them.

Melody touched Big Mat and was almost physically hurt by the intensity of the jealous rage he felt through him.

Big Mat said, "Git away from Chinatown. He got to learn to do for hisself."

Anna looked at Melody. He nodded. She got up and moved away. Chinatown began to moan in self-pity.

Big Mat shuffled about. At last he left the house and Chinatown's noises.

Melody listened to Chinatown and tried to think

of some help for his blind brother. The days were passing, and Chinatown seemed to be becoming less and less confident of himself. He had progressed to a point, then he had begun to slide back into helplessness. The only thing that quieted him was the feel of Anna's breast. Why was that? Maybe if Chinatown had a woman it would be good for him. That was something to think about. But who would sleep with a man with horribly dead eyes? Melody thought about that. But there must be a woman who needed money badly enough. He would find such a woman.

Without a word Melody left the house. He had been so long away from the whoring places that he did not know just which way to go. Finally he decided to stop at the bunkhouse and question some of the men. They might save him the search.

Melody kept a sharp lookout for trouble. But the streets were unusually quiet this afternoon. There were no children to be seen, and the vacant lots were empty. He wondered where the ball games were being played. In the Slav section of the town there were no young girls sitting on the porches. Most of the doors were closed. The day was hot. Except for an occasional face at a window, it was a dead town. But Melody was not fooled. The town was only playing dead. It had all the static violence of a crouching cat, a cat poised for a spring at some winged thing. The sound of the mills was unusually loud. It was a monotonous undertone through the still streets. At one corner there were broken beer bottles and rocks strewn about. A dried crust of black blood showed on a fence. There had been a fight. Some man had been hurt and had leaned against that fence for a minute. Then he had staggered off, or perhaps he had been carried. There were many strike posters along the way. Most of them had been covered by handbills printed by the mill interests. Melody saw that most of the handbills were written in two or more strange languages. He had been out of touch with recent developments in the town. But he needed no facts to tell him that something was going to happen soon. Something was going to be swift and bloody. The town spoke with the silence of a cocked rifle.

Most of the men in the bunkhouse were sleeping, but there was a little knot of dice players by the doorway. They looked up in surprise.

"Hallo," said Melody.

"Hallo," they answered.

"Boy, you got guts," said one of the men, "out walkin' today."

"What's the matter with today?" asked Melody.

The man laughed and rattled the dice.

"Ain't nothin' the matter with the day." He went back to playing.

"Yeah, it sure is a fine day." Another player laughed.

"Somebody killed maybe?" guessed Melody.

"Naw," said the first speaker, "but somebody gonna be killed."

"How come?"

"Where the hell you been? Man, today the day that the union give out its last word. If they don't git what they want they goin' to walk out sure this comin' Monday."

"Well, how come ever'body off the streets?"

"The mill owners ain't takin' no chances. They gittin' set ahead o' time. There a big trainload of armed deputies comin' in on the afternoon train."

"In a couple o' hours it be worth a man's life to walk outside," said one of the other players.

"Reckon I better git on back then," said Melody.

"Reckon so."

The game clicked on. Melody stood in the doorway, blocking the light. He was undecided.

One of the men said, "Git in or out."

Melody blurted, "Say, where the gals hang out now?"

"What gals?" asked the dice thrower.

"You know," he said, "the gals."

"You mean the good-time gals?"

"Yeah, that's what I mean."

"Well," said the man, "that's kinda hard to say."

"What you mean?"

"Most of 'em hangin' out in Pittsburgh, I reckon. There been too little money and too much trouble around town."

"Oh."

"Some places in Mex Town still goin'," somebody said.

"They lays for guys outside o' Mex Town," said the thrower. "Never catch me in there at dark."

The game went on.

"Well, much obliged," said Melody. He started away.

"Hey, wait a minute!" the dice thrower called. He passed the dice and walked outside with Melody. "You ain't a bad guy. I let you in on somethin' if you keep it quiet."

"Sure, I keep shut."

"Well, we don't want too many guys to be up there," said the man. "It's a good thing."

"Won't tell nobody," promised Melody.

"Okay then. You know that there dry-goods store out at the west edge o' town?"

Melody thought hard.

"You know," said the man. "Got a big square front. Only two-story buildin' around there."

"Oh yeah."

"Well, you go out there. Not in the front, mind. The steps to that second floor is on the outside o' the buildin', right up the side wall. Well, jest rap, and there you are."

"Much obliged."

"When you git out there you see why we want to keep it kinda to ourself." He gave Melody a twisted wink. "They ain't regulars. They town gals out to pick up some change."

Melody hurried on the way home. He had seen how the deputies acted around the mill. He did not want to be caught in the streets when they were patrolling the entire town. When those gunmen started beating heads with their gun butts they did not stop to ask which side you were on. They were like the posses he had seen in the South—they struck with blood lust, not wanting to quit until they had made a kill.

When he came in sight of the house he slowed his pace. He began to think about the dry-goods store at the west edge of town. It might be a good thing if Big Mat made a trip to that place.

Big Mat wanted to get as far away from home as possible. He started aimlessly walking. His feet were trained to a path and they led him toward the river. That was how he happened to see the new deputies come into town. Walking eight abreast along the river front, they did not swerve for any obstacle that could be kicked out of the way. They were, for the most part, men of indefinite age, neither young nor old. In their faces was a record of hard, undisciplined lives—old scars, broken noses, lantern jaws blued with stubble, lines of dissipation. They looked brutal because they had been brutalized. Each man carried a short club under his arm, the mark of his new trade. Most of them had been drinking; they were unnaturally quick of eye. Riotously they swung along, yelling at one another and laughing at nothing at all. They might have been headed for a party.

"Never thought I'd come to be a copper," one sang out.

"Don't take no pocketbooks. Remember you're knockin' heads for the law now," sang out another.

Big Mat swung far out of his way to avoid these men. He did not have sufficient strength in him to dispute the right of way. He was tired in body, but it was not fatigue that weakened him. Sapping him was that old frustration—the problem of Anna that seemed out of reach of his tough muscles. Now, added, was the frustration of his body, a sense of lost manhood, because of the unspent force in his loins. He turned and watched the men disappear into the town. Then he repeated his strange action of a past day: stooping, he lifted a big stone and walked along with it balanced in one palm.

That was when the sheriff saw him—a giant black man strolling along the river front, balancing a great rock in one hand. The sheriff had been standing with his foot on the running board of a car. There were two well-dressed men in the front seat. They turned at the sheriff's exclamation and looked with astonished eyes.

"God A'mighty! Do you see what I see?" asked the sheriff.

"Damn!" said the driver. "I hope he's one of our men."

"Think he's gonna throw that at somebody?" nervously asked the other man.

The driver stepped on the starter of the car.

"Wait a second," said the sheriff. He drew a revolver from under his coat. "Hey, you!" he called to Big Mat.

Big Mat stopped.

"Drop that boulder," he commanded.

Big Mat stared at them and held the stone.

The sheriff inched his gun forward. His face hardened.

"I said drop it," he snapped.

Big Mat raised the stone up and up. The sheriff's body quivered and then became like stone. His finger tightened on the trigger. The driver of the car kept his foot pressed on the starter of the car, although the motor had started. A tortured whine came from the engine. Then Big Mat tossed the stone away. It hit and sank slightly into the ground.

"Yessuh?" said Big Mat mildly.

The man sitting next to the driver gave a womanish laugh. The driver took his foot off the starter.

"Come over here," called the sheriff. He still kept the gun leveled.

Big Mat walked up to the car. The sheriff touched him lightly on the hips with his free hand. Then he stepped back and lowered the gun.

"What was you aimin' to do with that boulder?" he asked.

Big Mat searched for words. There were none. "Jest carryin' it, I reckon," was all he could say.

The driver of the car laughed.

"Just carryin' it, huh? That beats everythin' I ever heard."

The sheriff prodded Big Mat with the gun.

"Well, beat it and stay away from round here."

"Wait," said the driver. "You a steel worker?"

"Yessuh."

The sheriff pushed Big Mat again with the gun barrel.

"Just a minute, Sheriff," ordered the driver. "I'm running things here."

The sheriff put up his gun and touched his cap. But he continued to look steadily at Big Mat.

The driver said, "If this man is a loyal worker he can be a big help around here Monday."

His companion said, "Need all the good men we can get. Those deputies from Pittsburgh are all right, but it's not enough—not enough."

"You're not a striker, are you?" asked the driver.

"No suh."

"That's good." He said offhand to the sheriff, "You see?"

The sheriff scowled and fingered his gun butt.

"Now," said the driver, "what shift do you work?"

"Night shift. Day shift comin' up."

"Would you like four extra dollars a day?"

"Yessuh."

"Good." He turned to the sheriff. "Deputize this

man. Assign him his hours. He won't need a club. Just give him a couple of boulders. He'll earn his four dollars on Monday."

The sheriff touched his cap. The men waved to Big Mat and drove away. They were laughing.

"Sure is a mean trick to play on the union." They laughed.

The sheriff gestured for Big Mat to follow and started toward the mill gate. Big Mat stepped fast until he came abreast of him.

"This don't mean I got to stool-pigeon, do it?"

"Just you keep quiet and do what I say to do," snapped the sheriff.

A line of men were standing in front of an office. The sheriff placed Big Mat in the line. When Big Mat in his turn reached the office he was sworn in and his name added to a list. He was now a full-fledged deputy. He was to report for duty Monday afternoon. That would give him only a half day in the mills, but he was told that nothing would be deducted from his pay envelope on that account.

It had all been done so quickly that Mat could not organize in his head just what had transpired. He waited to one side for a favorable time to approach the sheriff. At last the sheriff appeared to be doing nothing, so Mat touched him on the arm.

"What the hell?—you again?" barked the sheriff.

"I was jest wonderin'——" began Big Mat. "I was jest wonderin' about this swearing in."

"What about it?"

"Jest what I swear to uphold?"

"Listen," said the sheriff, "you git on home. Monday you uphold what I tell you to uphold. That's all to it. Now git."

Big Mat went along the road toward home. He wondered what Melody would think of the entire business. It would probably be all right. They had not said anything about his having to tattle on his fellow workers. Anyway, he was a deputy. It was all down on the books. It could not be changed. He thought of the four extra dollars a day. That was a lot of money. Maybe he would buy Anna a lot of new clothes. Dance-hall dresses and shoes with high heels—she liked those things. It might make things right at home.

At a road intersection five men in overalls were arguing with one of the new deputies from Pittsburgh. The deputy threatened with his stick. He did not look to be a man for talk. The overalled men argued and kept their hands in their pockets.

"Ain't nobody allowed to crowd the street," the deputy was yelling.

A man answered, "Since when is five guys mindin' their own business a crowd?"

"I ain't gonna argue with you," yelled the deputy. "Them is the orders. Now break it up and git inside."

"This is still a free country. People can talk if they want to," said another man.

"That's what you think," said the deputy. "Now git along or take a taste of this here billy—whichever one you want."

The five men began to move slowly away. The deputy became impatient. With a curse he lashed one of the men across the back with the stick. The man staggered forward. His companions turned. For a minute it looked as though they might attack the deputy.

"Hoo-o-o! Riot!" yelled the deputy, backing against a wall.

A group of his fellows answered the call. With loud cries they rushed down on the overalled men. The five wheeled and scattered, running with the slow, ponderous tread of steel men.

One fled directly toward Big Mat.

"Stop him!" cried a couple of the deputies. Don't let him get away!" There was almost a sob in their voices.

The fleeing man saw Big Mat and stopped. For a second he hesitated, then with a bound he leaped a picket fence and was away on a tangent.

The two deputies did not attempt the fence. They stood sorrowfully looking after their escaped quarry.

"Damn! If we could just use our guns now," said one of them.

"There 'll be a chance," said the other. "This ain't over yet."

The first speaker suddenly remembered the big Negro standing so close. He nudged his companion. They came forward.

"Hey, you!" one cried.

"Me?"

"Yeah. Didn't you hear us holler to stop that fellow?"

"Yeah, I heard it."

"How come you didn't grab him?"

"He sprung over the fence."

"Oh, you a smart bastard! What's your name?"

"Mat."

"What else?"

"Moss."

"Okay, Mat Moss. What you doin' out of doors?"

"Jest come from the mill."

"Workin'?"

"Naw, they make me a deputy."

One of the men let out a great guffaw. The other began to snigger. It was a big joke.

"The laugh's on us," said one of them. "So you're a deputy too."

"Yeah, I reckon."

"Well, feller, you better tell it faster next time. We was jest about to paste you a couple of times for luck."

Big Mat nodded his head.

"I got to git on home," he said.

They walked back down the road with him.

"When you on duty?" asked one of the men.

"Starts in Monday."

"Yeah? That's gonna be a tough day."

"Guess so."

"Plenty of fun though." He gestured at his companion. "We got a bet on. Bet a week's pay I lays out more strikers than him."

"That's how come we was so sorry to miss that feller."

They stopped at the corner. Big Mat went on alone. He had only taken a couple of steps when one of them called.

"So long, pal. Just remember Monday that you're the boss in this here town. Anythin' you do is all right, 'cause you're the law. So don't take no back talk."

The nearer Big Mat got to his house the larger that thought loomed in his mind. The words began to take hold of him like a new green whisky, filling him with quick jubilation. All of his old hatreds came back and added flame to his feeling. He had been called "nigger" since childhood. "Nigger, nigger never die . . . " was the chant. The name that they gave to him had become a badge signifying poverty and filth. He had not been allowed to walk like a man. His food had been like the hog slops, and he had eaten. In the fields he had gone to the branch and gotten down on his belly. He had drunk his water like a dog left too long in the heat. They had taken his money and his women. They had made him run for his life. They would have run him with dogs through the swamps. They would have lynched him. He would have been a twisting torch. And he had escaped the South. Now here in the North he was hated by his fellow workers. He was a threat over their heads.

The women covered their faces at sight of him; the men spat; the children threw rocks. Always within him was that instinctive knowledge that he was being turned to white men's uses. So always with him was a basic distrust of a white. But now he was a boss. He was the law. After all, what did right or wrong matter in the case? Those thrilling new words were too much to resist. He was a boss, a boss over whites.

So Big Mat arrived at a kind of understanding. He would not be able to tell in words what it meant to be a deputy. But he could go home and strut before Anna.

Melody had been to the place above the dry-goods store at the west end of town. He had made all arrangements with the woman in charge. He was to bring Chinatown back with him on Monday night. The men would be occupied with the strike at that time. Chinatown must come and go without being seen. That was necessary. Trade might be lost by the sobering presence of a blind man.

Melody had not told Chinatown anything about the plan. It would be best as a surprise, he thought. Chinatown had so little confidence in himself. If he were told too soon he would have time to break himself with doubts.

However Melody did confide in Big Mat. He

had expected Big Mat to be caught up with the idea. Perhaps Mat would argue against it, he thought, and then end by making a trip to the west end of town himself. But Melody had been wrong. This was a different Big Mat these last days before the strike. This Big Mat was entirely taken up with his own idea—an idea that Melody could not share. They were out of tune with each other. For the first time Big Mat became inarticulate before his sensitive brother. All Mat could do was strut before Anna. And all he could say to Melody was:

"I sworn in as a sheriff's man now."

So each had to keep within himself. And when Monday morning came Big Mat went eagerly to the mills, and Melody stayed home. Melody knew that he would have to prepare Chinatown for what was to happen.

He had told Big Mat, "Don't care if they can me for missin' today. I got more important business than strikes on my mind. Chinatown come first."

All that morning Melody walked Chinatown. He wanted him to become used to being away from home. He told Chinatown that they had gone far into the town. But in reality they had walked a circle around and around the house. The town was too dangerous. Every street was patrolled.

But Chinatown believed that he had been from one end of the town to the other.

"I done good, huh?" he told Melody when it was finished.

"You done fine," said Melody. "Maybe this evenin' we try to walk out to the west end. That ain't
as far as where we been."

"Sure, that be easy," Chinatown said.

Melody smiled and was satisfied with this beginning. That afternoon he lay on his back and talked
about good times with his brother. Anna was an
eager listener.

"China, you 'member us and the gals?"

"What gals?"

"All the good-lookin' gals—Mexes, hunky gals,
gals down from Pittsburgh for the week ends."

"Yeah, them was pretty gals, all right."

"You was a stud hoss then."

"I sure was."

"They was always glad to see you come by."

"Onliest callin' card you need was green
money," said Chinatown. "An' ever' week I have
plenty o' them."

"You spend it all on dice and women and never
save a cent."

"Don't reckon I coulda stood it round here no
other way," he said. "Ever' week I git my pay and
start out. I was a big man with the gals, long as my
money hold out."

"Maybe you still a big man. They ain't forgit
Chinatown so easy—the biggest spender they ever
see."

"Ain't nobody want to look at me the way I is
now."

"That's where you wrong," said Melody.

"Why, I was walkin' out west end way jest a couple days ago. I meet some gals. The first thing they want to know is how come Chinatown don't come round."

Anna had been listening hard. At his mention of being at the west end of town she started violently. She had to close her startled eyes to hide her shock. Melody was too tense for Chinatown's answer to notice Anna. But Anna took no chance. She turned her back to him.

Chinatown wanted to believe.

"Aw, you jest funnin', Melody, ain't you?"

"Naw, I ain't funnin' at all. It's true."

"Who was it?"

"Oh, I dunno. Maybe some gals you musta give a break to once."

"They ain't heard about what happen to me. They ain't heard yet. That's it."

"Oh, sure they hear all about it," he said. "But that don't make no difference to them. They still say how come he don't come round."

Chinatown's permanent grin did not seem out of place now.

Melody said, "If you don't believe me, one good day let's us walk out there. I prove it to you."

"Aw, naw!" Chinatown grinned.

But Melody knew that the victory was almost won. He did not press the issue. He talked around the point, trying to make Chinatown suggest the trip himself. At last he did.

"Maybe if you ain't got nothin' better to do we

could walk that-a-way this evenin'," said Chinatown.

"Well, I dunno," pondered Melody.

"I could make it," cried Chinatown. "Didn't I
jest walk through the town and back, huh?"

"Well, I reckon it's all right," said Melody. "We
go 'bout nine."

Chinatown was shivering with excitement. He
managed to sit until five o'clock, then he asked
them for his good clothes.

"But it still light out," said Melody.

"Yeah, but I had oughta be ready."

They had to dress him. Anna pressed one of his
shirts and tried to dissuade them.

"The street is full of bad men," she said. "It is not
good time for going out."

"Where my tie? Where my tie?" asked Chinatown, fumbling at his throat.

She gave him the tie.

"Big Mat will not let this happen," she said.
"The blind one should wait for Big Mat."

"Is my shoes got a shine?" Chinatown wanted to
know.

"West end is a bad place. You should go east
end."

"But that's right through the heart o' town,"
said Melody. "We kin git to the west end without
goin' past them deputies."

"Somebody tell me that they are shootin' people
in the streets of the west end," said Anna.

"That ain't so," said Melody. "I was out there myself."

"Just the same, you should not go."

A thought came to Melody. It was a pleasant thought to have. He turned to Anna and held her by her arms. He thought she trembled a little in his grip.

"It ain't nothin' for me out there," he whispered in her ear. "This here is strictly Chinatown's party."

She twisted a little, but he held her closer.

"I ain't said nothin'," he told her, "but that don't mean I forgot you and that night us was together. Sometime I been near to bust, watchin' you ever' day, but I hold it back 'cause it ain't time yet. But one day you, me and Big Mat goin' to git straight."

He leaned down. She let her lips touch his. But her eyes were far away and worried.

To Chinatown, in his darkness, the minutes up to nine o'clock were like years. Every few minutes he would ask the hour. When told he would be astonished. It seemed incredible that the clock could creep so slowly. Once or twice he got the feeling that time must be moving backward.

When the clock said eight Chinatown was almost crazy with waiting. Melody was afraid to tell him the true time.

He told him, "Yeah, it's nine o'clock right now."

So he put black patches over Chintown's eyes

and left the house an hour ahead of time. They went through the dark back roads to the edge of town. Keeping on the outskirts, they began a circle westward. This was not the nearest way to the west end but it was the safest. The armed deputies stayed near the center of town.

Chinatown was worried now about his appearance. He began to question Melody.

"How my tooth? Don't feel like it's shinin'. All I got to depend on is that there tooth." He chattered on endlessly.

The dry-goods store had locked its doors long before, but little lights beckoned from the windows above. Melody waited until he was sure no one else was about, then he put Chinatown's feet on the narrow outside staircase. Chinatown struggled away from the helping hand at his elbow.

"Don't help me, less'n I ask for it," he told Melody.

So Melody did not touch him again. Chinatown mounted the steps, intense concentration in every nervous move. At the top he felt for the door and knocked. His sharp ears could hear the shuffle of carpet slippers somewhere inside. He straightened his back and turned down his hat brim.

A thin, sharp-eyed woman cracked the door less than an inch. She peered at Chinatown's shaded face.

"Who you want to see?"

"Tell the gals that Chinatown's come around." He handled his blind head as though he were see-

ing the woman. There was a good grin on his
mouth.

The woman peered at him again. She saw the
shadowy figure on the steps behind him. Melody
was making signs at her with his hands. She snorted.

"You got the wrong place, mister." She began
to close the door.

"It's me," spoke up Melody. "You 'member
me."

"Don't want no drunks around here."

Melody sprang in front of Chinatown.

"Wait a minute. I was here before. This my
brother I was tellin' you about."

The woman opened the door and let the light
fall in Melody's face. Recognition hit her eyes.

"Oh yes. Come on in."

Melody pulled Chinatown through the door.
The woman saw Chinatown's face.

She said, "So this here is the blind man you was
telling me about."

Chinatown's shoulders drooped and he grabbed
hold of Melody's arm. He began to swing his
black-patched face from side to side.

"Well, c'mon," beckoned the woman. "I got a
girl said she'd take him."

"Let's us go home, Melody. Let's us go home,"
pleaded Chinatown in a whisper. In that moment
he had become helpless again. He was close to tears.

But Melody led him down the long hall. The
woman stopped them at the last door. She opened
it without knocking and peered into the room.

Melody was standing to one side and could see a narrow section of a white iron bed.

"Got one here, honey," the woman said into the room. She turned to Melody. "All right, let him go in."

Chinatown would not release his grip on Melody's arm. He clung despite the nudges at his ribs.

Melody whispered fiercely, "Walk ahead—by yourself."

"I wants to go back," said Chinatown. He began to weep.

Melody dropped his hands to his side. He started to speak angrily to his brother, but the words did not come out. Then he made a little gesture to the woman.

"What's the matter?" she asked.

"Reckon I better take him back home," he apologized. "He ain't used to bein' out yet."

The woman drew her mouth into a hard line.

"This is what I get for lettin' a blind man in here in the first place."

"I'm sorry," said Melody.

"Get him on out of here," she snapped.

"C'mon, Chinatown," said Melody.

"Damn cheapskates comin' around here," mumbled the woman. She said to the unseen girl, "No sale, honey."

The girl came to the doorway. Her only piece of clothing was the flowered kimono that dragged the floor. She was a big-boned Slav girl with an honest face. Her hands were scrubbed red. Straw hair framed her slightly freckled face. A wad of gum popped endlessly in her jaws.

Melody looked quickly at her.

"Rosie!"

Zanski's granddaughter, Rosie. She stood there without surprise. She might have been resting on her feet behind the counter at the lunch wagon.

"Friends of yours, Rosie?" asked the little woman.

"Hallo," she said to Melody.

"I didn't know you was here," stammered Melody.

"Sure." She popped her gum and made a sign to the woman. "It's all right."

The woman walked away, grumbling.

Chinatown had his head on Melody's shoulder. He still clung onto the arm as though it were the only support in his darkness. The tears had stopped, but he continued to sniffle. He wiped his nose on Melody's coat.

"That's your brother got blinded when the blast went up?" she said.

"Yeah," said Melody. "Gonna take him home now."

"Bring him in here," she said.

"He don't want to."

"He needs to lay down for a little," she said. She came out and took Chinatown by the arm.

"C'mon, you need to rest just a second. Then you can go home." Her tone was easy and soothing.

Chinatown let himself be drawn forward. He

did look very tired. The emotional tensions he had
undergone had left him very near collapse. He sank
down on the bed and closed his eyes. Immediately
he was asleep. The black patches had slipped until
one rested across the bridge of his nose, the other
on his cheek. The light from the bed lamp shone
directly into his purple eye sockets.

The girl put a newspaper across the lamp shade,
darkening the bed. Then she took the newspaper
away.

"I forgot the light don't worry him."

Melody watched her with grateful eyes. This
was a good girl. He thought of Anna and her weeks
of patient nursing. So many like them were good
and kind. Why was that so? In his gratitude a
wave of emotion brought a lump in his throat, and
he thought that the only really good women he
had known were like these women.

"About ten minutes' sleep ought to fix him up,"
he said. "Then we'll git goin'."

Now he was ashamed of his purpose in coming
here.

The girl was not abashed. She still had a matter-
of-fact, everyday attitude.

"Ain't no need to hurry," she said, slumping
into a chair. "Wouldn't be no trade tonight. Everybody busy around the mill."

He sat down on the bed and put his hat on one
knee.

"Ain't been gittin' by the lunch wagon lately,"
he said. "Didn't even know you was gone."

"Oh, I'm still workin' there," she said. "Noticed you and your brothers didn't come in no more."

"You still workin' at the lunch wagon?" He could not keep the surprise out of his voice.

She laughed. "You think that's funny, huh?"

"Naw, naw, nothin' like that," he assured her.

"Well, it is kinda funny. Most all the other girls here work in the box factory in the daytime—come here at night."

"Yeah," he said.

It would not have been polite for him to voice his curiosity, but she knew of it through his face.

"You can't take home just eight dollars every week," she explained. "Not if everybody is gonna eat."

"What about the men in your family?"

"Ah-h-h . . ." She made a gesture. "They are all with the union. My brothers—they have not been on job since a month ago. They go crazy. But they got to stick by the union."

Melody thought of Zanski and his talk about his "kids." He wondered about the old man. Had his pride in his granddaughter soured, changing his entire outlook?

"I'm for the union too," she went on, "but all of the trade here comes from scabs and strike breakers. Nobody else got any money."

Melody was still thinking about Zanski.

"By the way, I ain't seen your grandfather. How he gittin' on?"

"He has taken to the bed," she said. "I don't

think he's gonna get up." She turned her face to the wall.

For a time he sat, not wanting to speak, a little afraid to move, for fear of disturbing her concentration on the wall. He knew that his mention of Zanski had upset her. He could have kicked himself, for he had known all along how Zanski would feel about his granddaughter.

He spoke hesitantly. "It ain't your fault. Don't feel bad."

She kept her face to the wall. He could barely hear her voice.

"I don't feel bad. It's the fault of them rotten scabs that us women got to bring the money in the house."

"I ain't quit the mill," he said, "but I ain't no scab."

He kept his head cocked for an answer, but she did not speak.

"You ain't mad at me?" he ventured.

She looked at him. Her gum began to pop.

"There ain't no sense in me bein' sore on nobody. Nobody 'd care if I was. Beside, that's the only thing good I got to tell the priest now on Sundays—that I ain't sore at folks."

"You goes to church ever' Sunday?"

"Sure."

"I ain't heard no preacher since I kin remember," said Melody.

"I ain't missed since—since when I had chicken pox. Was just ten years old then."

"My brother, Mat—he mighta been a preacher maybe. But me and Chinatown—we jest growed up bad."

"Church means more to me now," she said. Confessin' and all. I don't know how to say it, but it feels better to know that God's gonna punish me 'cause I'm bad."

"You ain't bad," he said.

"All the girls here go to church," she continued. "They like to confess."

"Reckon it's all right if they like it," he said.

She nodded at Chinatown. He stirred a little in his sleep, as if he felt her nod.

"He would feel better in the church," she said, and her hands made a movement as though she were molding a clay man.

"I heard tell of a blind preacher once," said Melody. "Used to recite the whole Bible in his head."

"There is a girl who works here some days. She talks about a blind man she's takin' care of. Says he goes off his nut. I tell her that he should be in the church, but she don't listen."

"This here blind preacher used to travel in Kentucky," said Melody. "I never seen him, but they say he'd git crazy and climb right up to the church rafters, tryin' to reach heaven."

"I tell her same as I'm tellin' you," she went on. "But I quit talkin'. She said she kept him plenty quiet by puttin' his hand inside her dress."

Melody stiffened.

"What you talkin' 'bout?"

"This girl," explained Rosie. "She says all the priest has got for the blind man to feel is beads."

"Who this girl?"

"I quit talkin' to her. Nobody can say that about the good priest."

"What's her name?" shouted Melody. He jumped to his feet.

The shout awakened Chinatown. He began to whimper.

Rosie was alarmed. Her words came quickly.

"I forget her name. She's a Mexican girl. I don't know anythin' about the man. I don't know any blind Mexicans."

There was a knock on the door.

A sharp voice called, "Any trouble in there, honey? Any trouble?"

Melody stood still. He waited.

Rosie said, "No, everythin's all right."

They could feel the woman listening outside. Then her slippered feet padded back along the hall.

"Knew them fellers was drunk," they heard her mumble.

"What's the matter with you?" asked Rosie. "You want to get me tossed out of here? She don't allow no rough stuff in her rooms."

Melody said quietly, "This here Mexican girl— she wears a dance-hall dress with beads all over. She got on high shoes with glass in the heels."

"You know her then?" said Rosie.

"Her name Anna," he said.

"That's her name, all right. She ain't been here in a week though."

So this was why Anna had been so anxious to stop their trip to the west end. Now that he knew, things in the past took on new significance. China-town had said something about her not being home to hear the rats at nights. Melody had not thought anything of it at the time. Now that he considered, it seemed unnatural that Anna should have been so satisfied with her arrangements at home. He should have known that such a woman would not be out of her man's bed unless there were some substitute.

Rosie was full of questions, but Melody cut her off.

"Looka here," he told her. "I got to go some-where quick. Can't take Chinatown. Kin he stay put for a coupla hours?"

"I don't know," she said.

"I'll be back and git him 'fore you know it." He took a five-dollar bill from his pocket. "Here. Jest leave him sleep till I git back."

She took the money and tucked it away under her kimono. Melody went over to Chinatown and pushed him flat on the bed.

"Go back to sleep," he told him. "I got to run out for a second."

Chinatown tried to cling onto his arm, but Melody jerked away. He could not hear his blind brother's whimperings now. He ran through the hall and down the outside staircase to the road. He had not closed the doors behind him. He knew that the sharp voice at the head of the stairs berated him. Then the door slammed.

Out in the road he hesitated a minute. He knew what he was going to say to Anna. But those words would not keep during the long trip around the edge of town. He broke into a run, heading homeward in a straight line. His feet hit the ground with confidence, for the moon had come up, making the night like day.

The workmen he passed on the road turned and stared. Then they watched narrowly for his pursuers. In a steel town men walked slowly, toting their aching shoulders. A running man must have deputies at his heels. A couple of deputies called out to Melody as he went by. They went a few steps after him and then gave up the chase. Once he saw a group of mounted men on the road ahead. He turned off, circling a hill. That new direction would take him a little out of the way, but he could not risk being stopped.

He had circled the hill and come into the section where most of the Slavs lived. Courtyards began to flash by. The women were on their front stoops to gape after the crazy man running, with nobody behind him. They fluttered their aprons. Deputies seemed to be everywhere. They were occupied with their job of keeping the streets clear. They did not bother to catch him. But a mounted trooper dogged his footsteps for a long way. He escaped by running through a narrow passage between a group of houses. But fright had helped waste his strength. He was winded. His breath whistling through his teeth, he leaned on a fence in front of a tar-papered house. A man peeped out of the door and began to jabber at him. Melody could not understand the words but he kept nodding his head. The man was still talking when he started to run again.

Melody had slowed to a fast walk when he reached the twisting road leading to his home. He had known that the big pile of ashes and garbage would be in his path, but now it seemed to hop suddenly in front of him. He was too tired to change direction and walk around it. It was better not to think but go straight ahead. He stepped into the soft stuff around the edges of the mound and struggled to the top. The brittle ashes broke under his feet. His muscles went soft and let him down. Only then did he realize how he had punished himself. The air was like fire roaring in his throat.

Then he saw Big Mat. He knew that big outline too well to be mistaken. From the opposite end of the street Big Mat was approaching the house. Melody got to his knees. His body struggled to rise. He slid aways down the mound. A tin can left a burning streak across one of his ankles.

For a long time Big Mat had been empty, like a torn paper sack inside. But all of that was over. He had begun to heal his ruptured ego with a new medicine. That medicine was a sense of brutal power. A few careless words from a police deputy had started that strange healing. This Monday would complete the cure. That the cure might be deadly was too deep a thought for him. The only thing he felt was a sense of becoming whole again.

So that Monday morning when he started for the mills he did not hear Melody say, "I got more important business than strikes on my mind. China-town come first." Big Mat hardly remembered Melody and Chinatown. He knew that something had been said about the west end of town and a dry-goods store where there were town gals, but all that meant nothing today.

Today he would be the law—the boss. . . .

As yet Big Mat had not seen any real action. There he was in the mill, working as always. It seemed as though his short time on the job would never end. This day the men could not carry on the making of steel as they had in the past. There was a mere skeleton force trying to keep the fur-naces from growing cold. Big Mat rushed from place to place with a squad of experienced men. However, it was impossible to protect all of the fires. Some of the furnaces had to be abandoned.

The effectiveness of the strike against the fur-naces astounded Big Mat. Men had done this thing to these seemingly eternal fires. Now these mon-sters that made metal were dependent upon the strength of Big Mat. It moved him to rush madly about the yards, knowing that only his will would keep a fatal crack from their big, brittle insides.

Still he was glad when his half day was through.

He would get more than his fill of action before it was over, the sheriff had told him. As yet there had been no serious trouble. A little fight at the mill gates—nothing to speak of. But things were bound to break open to hell and back. Big Mat's only instructions were to keep the streets clear of mobs. One man standing still on the street was a mob. No telling what a man might do if he were given a chance to stand and think.

At the mill gates Big Mat saw the signs of bloodshed. There had been a fight. Placards were broken, and there was splintered wood lying in dried blood. Those stains, now turning black, trailed away, drop by drop, as though men with bloody heads had risen off the ground and run a distance.

A man told Big Mat what had happened.

"Wasn't more 'n two, three hour ago. I was jest about to git down off the trolley. I seen some guys walkin' up and down in front of the mill gate. They was carryin' them signs." He pointed around the ground. "You see the way they're broken now. Well, them mounted troopers did that. Man, it was awful! I tell you I run back in the trolley car and stayed there. Wouldn't 'a' been so bad, only them strikers tried to stay and talk. Called them police 'cossacks.' Said somethin' 'bout havin' the right to picket. Kept talkin' 'bout their rights. Heads was busted like ripe cantalopes. I jest now git up nerve to come to work. Ascared them troopers might come back and think I was one o' the union."

Big Mat had a chance to see some of those mounted state troopers. He was at his post along the river-front road when they came riding: two men on fine horses. They carried themselves well—straight backs and a firm seat in the saddle. In their hands were the familiar short clubs. They passed Big Mat. He saw their faces. They were hard, lean faces. These troopers were boys. They did not look as if they knew anything but pride in a uniform and a strong horse.

An hour later those two came riding back. This time they were swinging the short clubs. Before them ran a group of strikers and their women. The mounted troopers wielded the clubs like men with scythes, felling grain. There was a fierce, almost religious ecstasy in them as they landed blow after blow. Their horses were a part of them. These beasts were trained to run down human beings. A woman who had fallen escaped the deadly hoofs, but the trooper wheeled his mount and made good at the second try. She lay on the ground grinding her hands in the dust, the better to take the pain of a broken hip.

Big Mat found himself maneuvering with the other deputies to trap the terrified strikers. Taking his place in a half circle of men, he helped drive the bloody group into a blind alley. It was in this drive that Big Mat made complete kinship with the brutal troopers.

It was the terror in the strikers that brought him to that final kinship. A man had tried to break through the half circle and had run full tilt into Big Mat. With one sweep of his arm he had sent the man flying back at his fellows. The man's body had shouted its terror. People had cried out at the look on Big Mat's face. He had always been the man to slaughter animals, and now these people became merely frightened animals. They might have been chickens. He might have gathered a bunch of them under his arm, pulled off their heads and watched them flop about the road. The absolute terror in these people made him feel like flinging himself on their backs and dragging them to the ground with his teeth.

With the strikers huddled, sheeplike, at one end of the blind alley, the deputies had to stop fighting. Standing glaring at their victims, they were like men regretful at the finish of an orgasm. They released the women but they held the men and gave them a last word: "Go to the mill or go to jail." Most of the strikers chose the jail, but some of the foreigners were frightened into returning to the job.

And throughout the evening it was the same— Big Mat going from place to place, spreading terror among the passive people, giving them the ultimatum: "To work or to jail." He was with the troopers when they rode their horses into the houses of the Slavs. He was there when a union organizer was caught and beaten. After the beating they had to look at the man's feet to know which way the face turned. The back and front of the head had become bloody twins. Big Mat had held men and knocked their heads together. He had attacked those people who wanted nothing more than to reach their homes in safety. He had drunk out of the deputies' bottles until he was blind with whisky and power. Like the deputies and troopers, he no longer needed reasons for aggression. Cruelty was a thing desirable in itself.

That night the sheriff himself came and slapped Big Mat on the back. This new deputy had done well—the sheriff made that clear.

"Gonna put you on full time," he said. "You got talents for this here business."

Big Mat had learned something else from the troopers—he made a clumsy salute.

The sheriff laughed.

From someplace in the night came the call: "Riot! . . . Ho-o-o! Riot!"

Big Mat started forward. His eyes were shining and eager. He pulled the sheriff several feet before he felt the detaining hand on his arm.

"Damn!" cried the sheriff. This big black man made him a little nervous. The muscles under his touch were electric. "Let them guys handle their own trouble. I got somethin' else for you."

And Big Mat had his head turned regretfully toward the sounds of struggle and flight.

"What you want me to do?"

"First you better git a bite to eat," said the sheriff. "You been on all day."

"Ain't hungry," said Big Mat.

"All the same, you eat," commanded the sheriff. "I'm the guy in charge here."

"Yeah."

"You come right back though." He poked Big Mat in the ribs and spoke in a whisper. "Tonight we goin' to raid the union headquarters."

Big Mat started for home but he was not going to eat. This night he would have it out with Anna. He had handled people, and they feared him. Their fear had made him whole. Now he would go to Anna a whole man. She would fear him too. Now all of the doubt and indecision of the past seemed a ridiculous thing. Now he had a new slant on life. At one time he had wondered why men were violent against him. Now he knew that in this world it was kick or be kicked. From this moment on he would be the kicker. Anna should know that he was a new man. She should know that he was a boss.

A memory came to him of Kentucky and old Mr Johnston. If there had been humor in Big Mat he might have laughed out loud. What would Mr Johnston, the master of plantations, say about all this? What would he think of his former debt slave now? And the riding boss—he should stand for a moment here in Big Mat's path. It would be the same as their last meeting. And Big Mat would not run in fear this time.

But there was no Mr Johnston now, and the riding boss was far away. He felt a keen regret.

Melody sat very still at the bottom of the ash pile and watched Big Mat go to the house. There would be no opportunity to see Anna alone now, he thought. He got to his feet and dusted the ashes out of his clothes. He wiped his sweat-and-dust-caked face on the tail of his shirt. Then he walked to the door. It would only take a minute to say what he had to say. Perhaps that minute would come if he waited.

Big Mat was washing his hands in kerosene. Already he had dipped them five times in the kerosene. It seemed to him that they needed no more of that washing, but yet he was not satisfied. From under heavy brows he looked up at Melody. He was annoyed that his brother had come in.

"Hallo," mumbled Melody.

" 'Lo," he answered.

Melody's eyes steadied. There was Anna at the stove, dressed as though she were figuring on going someplace. A ribbon held her hair straight down her back. She had on a pink beaded dress and new rhinestone shoes. When she moved in front of the stove the beads glittered and clicked and light struck, matchlike, on the rhinestones. It would have been good to see if he hadn't been so full of what he wanted to say.

When he spoke to her she did not bother to answer or turn.

"Thought China was with you," said Big Mat.

"Left him at the place," he told him. "China all right."

He sat down on the cot to wait, keeping Anna in his eye. There was the sound of Big Mat scrubbing at his hands. The splashing of the kerosene sounded loud in the room. Then Melody began to feel the pain of the cut across his ankle. But he fixed his mind in a vise and did not look down.

Years passed before Big Mat washed his hands in water and rubbed them dry on the seat of his pants. Then he started out the back door, unbuttoning his overalls.

Melody held himself tense, straining to hear the creak of the outhouse door. When it came he sprang to his feet. The cot bounced off the floor.

Anna whirled around. There was a strained look about her. Fright was in her eyes.

"What——?" she began.

"Rosie told me," he whispered. "Rosie told me."

She edged sidewise until the table was between them.

"Rosie told me," he whispered again.

"You are sick?" Her nervous eyes kept flickering at something underneath the cot. "It is the heat."

"You was out whorin'." He came toward her. "Rosie told me."

"Oh?" She seemed relieved—as though she

had been afraid he was going to say something else.

"Say it's a lie," he pleaded.

Turning her back, she moved her hands among the pots.

"I ain't carin' what happened," he said. "I want you to say it's a lie."

Over her shoulder she looked at him queerly.

She said, "It's a lie."

"Naw, it ain't! Naw, it ain't!" he cried.

"Quiet! Mat will hear," she cautioned.

He tried to take hold of her. The things he wanted to say came out in a rush.

"Look, I know why you done it. You ain't doin' no good with Big Mat. It's made you crazy like him and me."

She struggled out of his hands, rocking the lighted lamp on the table.

"I talk to you tomorrow," she whispered. "Mat come back now."

He stood stock-still, his head inclined toward the back door. No sound but the wind and the mills. Quickly he voiced the thought that had come to him back there in the little room above the dry-goods store.

"Let's you and me run off—go someplace where Big Mat won't never find us. I git me a job and make money. I git you ever'thin' you want. You won't need nobody else but me."

He would have gone on talking, but she broke in:

"I see you tomorrow."

"Tell me now."

"Not now. You wait."

"I can't wait around no more," he cried. "I got to know now."

"Go away," she said. Then she tried to soften those words. "Tomorrow maybe I say yes."

He knew she was just playing along with him. The blood pounded behind his eyes.

"You got to go. I fix it so you can't stay here. I tell Big Mat you was out hustlin'."

"Pah!" She dry-spit at his feet. "I am sick of you. You talk big but do nothin'. You break wind with your mouth."

"I tell Big Mat."

"It is like when I first see you. Nothin' but dreams come out of your head. You are not man."

"You lay down with me once," he told her.

"I never tell I lay with you," she said, "because you are nothin' but sissy feller who like woman."

Then he forgot to keep his voice lowered.

"I tell Big Mat," he cried out. His own voice froze him.

In the silence the heavy step at the back door was another loud noise. Big Mat stood there.

He said, "Tell me what?"

Melody could not make a sound, could not move away from the table. Big Mat went to Anna and stood over her.

"Tell me what?"

"Some girl say——" Her voice broke. "He tell big lie," she said, pointing at Melody.

Big Mat motioned for her to keep talking.

"He say I meet feller in house," she finished.

Big Mat turned. What Melody saw in his brother frightened him.

"Rosie say it. It was Rosie," he blurted out.

The flat of Mat's hand across her face was like a butcher slapping wet meat. She sat down heavily on the floor.

"That what been the matter," he said. "I knowed it."

She did not try to lie. Drawing her legs under her, she sat there. Her eyes seemed to say, "What has to happen has to happen. I can't do any more."

"That's how come you don't lay with me no more," he said. "Your mind on somebody else."

She would not look up at him.

"Who this other guy?" cried Big Mat.

Anna did not answer.

For a second he stood there at a loss. Then he hooked a hand under one of her armpits and jerked her upright. She hung on his hand like a rag doll, one shoulder high, one toe touching the floor. Now he thundered with the full strength of his body:

"Who he?"

Her head flopped to one side. It seemed as though she were looking straight at Melody. Again he was frightened for himself.

"Mat kill any creeper," his voice pleaded.

"Who he?" thundered Big Mat. It would have been impossible not to answer him.

She spoke slowly. "Two, three weeks I go out to

house. I lay with any feller got money. I don't ask no feller no name."

Melody sank back across the table.

Big Mat was unbuckling the heavy leather around his waist. That belt was two inches wide. His name was fixed with brass studs in the leather.

"Mat, what you fixin' to do?" But even as he spoke Melody knew.

Big Mat spoke to Anna.

"You ain't gonna look good to the next guy." The heavy leather was running through his fingers.

Melody tried to close his eyes.

Anna screamed, "Kill me! It is the only way I stay here." Then she jerked away and ran to the cot. Fishing under it, she pulled out a paper suitcase. "See—tomorrow you would come here, and I am far away." The lock sprung, and her clothes tumbled out on the floor.

Big Mat started toward her.

"You think I lay with lotsa feller because I whore?" she cried.

The brass-studded belt dangled ready in his hand.

"You think I like these feller?" Her nervous fingers were working her dress around straight.

His arm came back until the shoulder muscles bunched.

"No, I do it for money to go from peon like you!" she screamed. "In Mexico peon on ground. Here peon work in mill."

Big Mat's muscles knotted, and the belt snapped down. A shoulder strap of the beaded dress parted under the leather. Beads fell to the floor like rain on a tin roof.

"You are a peon," she kept on. "I will not live with peon." Her body shook as the belt dragged across it. She was out of her senses, the way she kept talking. "You are not *Americano. Americano* live in big house back in hills." The crack of the whip made little stops in among her tumbling words. "*Americano* have big car." She went to her knees under the wild lash. "They are not peon like you."

The heavy sweat misted off of Big Mat's face when his head jerked under the force of the blows. His shirt was like black skin.

Outside, from the road, a high voice began to scream, "Bloody murder!" It sounded like Sugar Mama. Nobody else could scream like that without seeming to pause for breath. The voice outside grew wilder and wilder every minute, but nobody came in to stop Big Mat. Folks in this part of town would go into their houses and close the doors when trouble started.

Through the noise from outside Melody could barely hear Anna.

"You are dirt—goat dropping—not Black Irish—black peon."

Big Mat went hog wild and laid the belt across her face.

Back in Kentucky the kids had sung, "Nigger, nigger never die, black face and shiny eye." Those words turned over and over in Melody's head.

Anna had buried her face in her arms, but he brought the belt up from the floor. Still she was trying to keep on talking. Her words turned into blood bubbles.

There was shadow in that house, but Melody could see the welts grow, the belt falling again to leave them gray, the little ragged lines of red running into the dress bunched at her waist. Blood sickness swam through him. He closed his eyes and used his arms to shut out sound. But a little bile slid between his shut teeth. For a long time he waited. Then at last the bang of the door came to his closed ears. He looked up.

Big Mat had gone suddenly. Anna was a figure crouched head to knees. She was dead looking. Melody's mind fastened on little things: the lamplight, the beads on the floor, the rhinestone shoes. In the lamplight the beads and rhinestones were picked with red. Red curls of skin covered her naked back. Except where her hair made a black covering for her face she might have been sprinkled with beads and rhinestones.

He sat still, not moving when Sugar Mama came like a furtive dog into the house. He watched Sugar Mama lift the girl's head. There was no passion in the cut face. Sugar Mama worked quickly. She went to the shelf and got the lard can. She began to spread the lard across the whip cuts. All the time she kept her big dog's eyes rolling toward the door, as though fearful of Big Mat's return. She did not wait to do much more. A light coat thrown over the larded back, the suitcase and a pair of shoes, and she was taking Anna out through the doorway.

Melody did not call out or try to follow them. Like a man in a dream, his attention was compelled by two bright objects in the center of the room. They were the rhinestone shoes. Anna had gone away and left the shoes with high heels behind. They held his eyes and mind. In a strange way they were conclusive.

Big Mat ran from the house, dragging the red-stained belt. He was still in his madness, not daring to relax. Relaxation would have brought the truth to him, and he did not want to know the truth. He did not want to know that Anna had beaten him finally, that all of his new-found power had been useless against her will. So he hurried along the road, keeping his madness red in his mind by repeating a word to himself:

"Peon . . . peon . . . peon . . ."

Clear to the river front he went, repeating his word. He was looking for the sheriff. There was to be a raid on the union headquarters, and Big Mat had to be among the raiders. Only new violence could strengthen him, restore his feeling of power. That feeling must come quickly, or the cracks that Anna had cleaved would widen until he was nothing but the pieces of a man.

The sheriff and his band were waiting. They

would not have gone without Big Mat. He was to be the key figure in the attack. They were worried until they saw him coming along the road. The sheriff poked a deputy in the side.

"See?" he crowed, pointing toward Mat. "What I tell you?"

A deputy said, "Yeah, he's comin', all right, but that don't mean he's goin' to do it."

"He'll do it. Jest wait and see."

"Well, I wouldn't do it by myself. I wouldn't."

"Me neither," said another man. "Them union guys is desperate now."

One of the troopers grinned.

"I might do it but I'd want more than my horse with me."

The sheriff hailed Big Mat.

"Hallo! Thought you wasn't comin' back. What held you up?"

Big Mat made a gesture with his hands.

"Okay," said the sheriff. "All ready to go?" He did not wait for an answer. "Now here's the plan. We got to have some guy go in there and start trouble first. You catch it, jest the old stuff—knock a few guys down; kinda start a riot. Then before anything can happen we bust in and cart off the whole shebang for disturbin' the peace."

"You're goin' to go in first." The trooper laughed.

The sheriff gave the trooper a hard look, then turned to Big Mat.

"Well, that's it," he confessed. "Think you can handle it?"

Big Mat turned toward the center of town. The sheriff mistook the gesture.

"Wait!" he said. "You can't go back on your oath like this. You're a sworn deputy. Ain't no yellow bellies in my outfit."

"I was jest gittin' started," said Big Mat.

He strode back down the moonlit road.

The sheriff called:

"Jest walk in like you was goin' to sign up. We won't be far behind."

"Damn, he's game!" said the trooper.

"Seem like he's kinda anxious to go," marveled the sheriff. Then he became businesslike. "Well, c'mon, you guys, let's git started. But don't crowd him too close."

Big Mat walked alone in the center of the road. The houses on every side were dark but they were full of hidden life. The deputies patrolling their beats came to look but they knew him and turned away. The dogs scrapping over the garbage in the road stopped their snarling at the menace of his steady footsteps. The clank of the mills was subdued and disjointed but it was there as always. Everything that the town had known was still there, but Big Mat was utterly alone. His was a terrible concentration as he walked along, dragging the red belt through the dust.

Peon . . . peon . . . that was what she had called him. He knew the term. The Mexicans around here used it. It was for slaves bound on the soil—slaves bound on the job. There were no white peons. It was a term like "nigger." He could not understand just why he had been called by that name, but the contempt behind it was real. His new-found power had had no strength against that contempt. Maybe in the South he had been just a peon. There had been a riding boss to count the drops of sweat from his body. But here there was no riding boss. He had to keep saying it to himself: there was no riding boss . . . there was no riding boss. . . .

It was bad, trying to keep from thinking all that long way to the union headquarters. The cracks in his ego were widening. He hurried his steps.

The union headquarters were just a desk and a few chairs in a store front. Behind that desk sat a calm, square-faced man, the organizer for the district. Women occupied the chairs. Their men stood against the wall. There was no air of great activity here. There was, rather, the feeling of purposeful waiting. For these men and women knew that they were to be raided. The news had leaked out through one of the drunken deputies. A youth kept watch at the front door. He called back to the man behind the desk:

"Ain't nobody yet, sir."

"Just keep lookin', boy. They'll be here."

The boy turned his anxious eyes toward the glass.

A couple of women started talking under their breath to a big, hairy fellow. Their words were foreign, but their fear spoke plainly. The big-bearded man shook himself. His coat rattled like paper. Everybody looked.

The organizer cleared his throat to command attention. He spoke.

"Say, did I ever tell you folks 'bout the time I was weldin' in Monessen? I was nothin' but a kid. There I was doin' a man's job. My old man taught all his boys the trade, you know."

Everybody was hanging on his words. He might have been telling them how to win the strike.

"My old lady run a boardin'house—took in all the metal workers that 'd pay three bucks a week and took in all that couldn't. Wasn't always that way, but there was a fire on a trestle, and my old man got himself burned some. So I had to do the weldin'. And there had to be boarders."

The boy turned his strained eyes.

"Ain't nobody yet."

"Well," the organizer said, "they wanted to know how old I was when I got the job. So of course I tried to lie a little—was pretty big for my age."

One of the women said:

"Look, we know they're comin'—we know that. Then why don't you let our men go home? We don't want no more trouble. We don't want no more trouble."

Another woman broke in:

"My boy's laid up now. I don't want my man to get hurt. Why don't we just leave?"

Her man said:

"Look, you go home, Sally. You go home."

The organizer looked at her.

"We ain't breakin' the law. This is an organization under the law. How long do you think we'd last, runnin' and hidin' like criminals?"

Nobody said anything.

"Nobody yet," droned the boy at the glass.

"As I was sayin'," took up the organizer, "I had to lie a little 'bout my age. Said I was nineteen. The boss called me a liar right off. He knew I couldn't be over fifteen. But I knew my weldin', so he hired me. 'Of course,' he told me, 'on account of your age we got to give you a boy's job instead of a man's.' That was all right with me, so I asked him what was the difference in hours between a man's job and a boy's job. 'Ain't no difference in hours,' the boss told me. 'The difference is in pay. Boys just get half as much.' "

A woman said:

"Why don't they come?" She wrung her hands.

The organizer started another story.

"Say, did I ever tell you folks 'bout——?"

The boy at the window broke in. His voice went into falsetto.

"A man's comin'! Big fella—black. . . ."

One of the men walked to the window.

"Yeah, that's them, all right. Seen that big guy before. He's a bad one."

The organizer motioned to the boy at the window.

"Go on out the back way, son. You done good."

"I don't mind stickin'."

"Naw, you go on," the organizer said.

The boy left.

Big Mat stopped outside of the window and looked in. He saw a place full of calm people, a square-faced man sitting behind a desk. All of these people were intent upon themselves. They did not look up at his terrible face on the pane. He hesitated a minute before he walked in.

Inside, he stood tensed for action. The bellows of his chest worked up and down, making loud whistling noises. But nobody spoke to him or paid him the least attention. A man moved against the wall, and Big Mat spun suddenly. But the man had only shifted, folding his arms, his coat crackling like newspaper.

Big Mat became tired of his tense position. But how could he let down? How was he going to start trouble? He could not just walk up and hit people who were calmly looking at the floor. His eyes began to shift out toward the street. The sheriff would know what to do. But the sheriff and his men were out of sight. So Big Mat stood in the center of the floor, unable to fight or to leave. He was trapped by the calmness.

The still minutes ticked by. Big Mat shifted from foot to foot. At last, in desperation, he started forward. The man behind the desk did not look up but extended his hand with a slip of paper. Big Mat took the paper and held it. He watched the people around him. If only someone would say something, look at him, help him by their fear to do the thing he had come to do.

The man behind the desk looked up for an instant and beckoned toward a stub of a pencil. Big Mat felt his hand forced toward the desk. In another minute he might have signed a union blank, but a woman broke under the tension.

"He's a deputy! He's a low-down deputy! He didn't come here to sign."

That was all he had wanted. With his foot he kicked the desk over on the union organizer. Then he was beating his way through the crowd. The people stampeded out of the store front. A little gray Slav came under Big Mat's hands. Those hands fastened around the old man's neck. Hardly realizing that he carried a man, Big Mat broke through the doorway and into the road.

The sheriff and his men were waiting.

Big Mat stood out in the night, breathing in the air that intoxicated him like ether. Peon . . . peon . . . He was no peon. There was no riding boss over him now. He turned wildly and gazed at the mill. A great exhilaration almost swept him into the air. The townsfolk were down. He was exalted. A bitterness toward all things white hit him like a hot iron. Then he knew. There was a riding boss— Big Mat. Big Mat Moss from the red hills was the riding boss. For the first time in his life he laughed aloud. Laughing crazily, he held the man by the neck.

The old Slav struggled feebly in Big Mat's great hands. He cried out against the hands of Big Mat, the black riding boss. He had never been in the South. He was from across the sea. His village was in the Ukraine, nestling the Carpathian mountains. From that great distance he had come to be crushed by hands that had learned hate in a place that did not exist in his experience. He slid out of those hands, and his gray little body barely made a mound on the level ground.

The mounted troopers galloped up and down the street, leaning over their horses' necks to club the fleeing men and women. But Big Mat did not see them. He looked at the mills, a string of broken lights now. So many of the fires that had seemed eternal were now gone.

Big Mat looked at the mills, and the big feelings were lifting him high in the air. He was big as God Almighty. The sun was down, or his head would have thrown a shadow to shade the river front. He could have spit and quenched a blast furnace. Big Mat's eyes were big as half-moons. They stretched, and their full size showed white all around black pin points. His mind went rocketing at a crazy speed. All of his life here at the mills flashed before him for an instant. Smothers had been a liar. Steel couldn't curse a man. Steel couldn't hurt him. He was the riding boss. How could those dead mills touch him? With his strength he could relight their fires or he could let them lie cold. Without Black Irish they were dead.

This was the only place for a big black man to be.

The blow on the back of his head took him without warning. His eyes had been the measure of the whole river front. His big eyes could not have seen the young Slav and the pickax handle. He did not fall. He staggered about like his blind brother in search of the outhouse. The blows fell again and again. Still he did not fall. His hands groped for his assailant. He had been tuned to the pitch of madness, but the instinct of self-preservation forced his mind down the scale to a more normal pitch. He was blinded by that long slide.

Like a reflection in disturbed water, the face of the young Slav came into his vision. He looked at that face from a great distance. It would only be a moment before he must crash to the ground. His eyes were objective. He had all the objectivity of a man who is closer to death than life. From that dark place he looked back at the world. This is what he saw:

A young man, a Zanski without the handle-bar hairs underneath his nose, a young Slav frantic because he was killing a man. A good face, a little crazy and twisted with repugnance for the blows he must deal.

He, Mat, was the riding boss, and hate would give this club hand the strength it needed.

His vision faded. He was confused. It seemed to him that he had been through all of this once before. Only at that far time he had been the arm strong with hate. Yes, once he had beaten down a riding boss. A long time ago in the red hills he had done this thing and run away. Had that riding boss been as he was now? Big Mat went farther away and no longer could distinguish himself from these other figures. They were all one and all the same. In that confusion he sensed something true. Maybe somewhere in these mills a new Mr Johnston was creating riding bosses, making a difference where none existed.

The young Slav danced about and used the pickax handle. Because the big black man did not fall he was filled with terror. Because the little eyes seemed to regard him so calmly he had to become frenzied to finish the job. So he danced about. and the sound of the blows was dull. It was like a Punch and Judy show, the way the black head wagged under the stick. It was funny, funny without laughter.

The mounted troopers swept back down the street. They passed two bodies—an old Slav's and Big Mat's. . . .

Later at the jail, the sheriff, in his own way, summed up the whole thing.

"Sure is a shame that big nigger had to go and git himself killed. But I don't reckon we can pin it on nobody. Just accidental in the line o' duty, that's all. He was game, all right, but crazier 'n hell. That's the thing 'bout nigger deputies—they're fightin' the race war 'stead of a labor strike. Always be like that, I guess, as long as they come from the South. There 'll be somebody to take his place, an' that there's one reason why the union ain't gonna win. They didn't figure on the South when they started this here. . . ."

Melody and Chinatown had been through much since they left Kentucky one early spring night. And now they were leaving the mills. They were at the station, waiting for the train. The months behind them stood out like years. Winter was coming. . . . That morning there was a thin film of ice in quiet places along the Monongahela. The sun came out and lanced that thin ice, leaving it pitted with black holes. The Indian summer was gone. The strike had gone with the Indian summer, destroyed by forces cold and ruthless. Now the mills had more men than they needed. Wages were down.

But that was not why Melody was taking Chinatown away. There was a deep pain in Melody. He was never happy. He thought about the first months in the Allegheny Valley. Then he had been fearful of the greatness around him, the endless clash of big forces playing up and down the banks of long rivers. This place had been a monster, beautiful in an ugly strength that fascinated a man so that it made him sing his fear. It was a new, big world. Right now all of Melody's world was a little, dull pain. He had left his guitar behind.

Someday, Melody thought, he and Chinatown would go home to Kentucky. But he did not think about that very hard. He was beginning to feel the truth: they would never go home. Now they would go to Pittsburgh.

Many Negroes had gone to Pittsburgh before them; many were castoffs of the mills. They had settled in the bottoms of that city, making a running sore at those lowest points. But a man had told Melody where to live: the Strip, a place where rent was nearly free and guys who knew how to make out would show them the ropes. That was good. Melody had a check for two hundred and fifty dollars in his pocket, but that did not seem like big money now. It was the little price that had been paid for Chinatown's eyes.

The train roared in. The sides and flickering windows of the black coaches became steady in his eye. He took Chinatown's arm and helped him aboard. The whistle sounded twice—highball. They were on the way.

It was just like any other passenger train but to Melody it was special. This train was the one taking him away from the mills . . . Anna . . . Chinatown's eyes . . . Big Mat's grave. . . . The only things he carried of these were a homemade watch fob and an old backless Bible.

They took seats in the smoking car. Melody did not look out of the window. He looked at the black man in the seat across from them. That man wore an old khaki uniform and a wrinkled overseas cap. Under that cap an elastic band held two black patches over the soldier's eyes. Melody looked from the soldier to Chinatown. Two blind men facing one another, not knowing.

"Anybody in front of me got a smoke?" asked the soldier.

"Sure." And Chinatown pulled out his pack of cigarettes.

Miraculously they made the exchange.

"You ain't a doughboy?" asked the soldier.

"Naw, steel worker," said Chinatown.

"I'm just from the soldiers' hospital. I'm well now, so I'm goin' on down the line to my folks."

"We goin' to Pittsburgh."

"Used to be a steel man myself 'fore the war."

They talked along many of the long miles to Pittsburgh. Finally they were friendly enough for Chinatown to ask:

"How come you quit the mills? What was the sense goin' somewhere to git shot?"

"Oh, I dunno," said the soldier. "It was just one day I was standin' outside the mill to git the cool river air, and the feelin' come on me."

"Yeah?"

"The feelin' was sorta like that river air, I guess. Ain't no sense tellin' it to quit blowin'. It don't care if you want to git cool or not."

Chinatown laughed.

"Yeah, but I kin go in the house an' shut down the windows if I git tired o' that air."

"There's one thing I couldn't shut out."

"What was that?"

"Listen."

Chinatown cocked his head to one side. He heard only the noises of the train.

"You hear it?" asked the soldier.

"Naw, I can't hear nothin'."

"There, it soundin' off again!" he cried. "Hear it? Boom! . . . Boom! . . . Boom! . . ."

The sound was real to the soldier. For him it was beating regularly, like the bass in a band, faint and traveling slowly on the breeze, long drawn out, as though too heavy a load to be carried on the wind. To him it was like a big drum somewhere in the valley. He did not know that the drum had stopped beating months ago. He would always hear a drum.

"What I'm supposed to be listenin' for?" asked Chinatown. "The train drown out ever'thin'."

"Guns," he said. "It's guns."

"Who be shootin' off guns round here?"

"Them guns is far away. Maybe a hundred miles."

"Can't no gun sound that far."

"Them is cannon guns, bigger 'n a smokestack."

"Damn, not a mill stack!"

"Yeah."

Chinatown strained his ears. They had become very good ears since his eyes had gone. He strained so hard that he heard the guns. Their noise came over the rumble of the train.

"Sound like somethin' big an' important that a fella's missin', don't it?" asked the soldier.

Chinatown nodded.

Melody watched the nod. He looked at the two blind men closely. Their heads cocked to one side, listening for sounds that didn't exist. They were twins.

WILLIAM ATTAWAY was born in Greenville, Mississippi, in 1911 and moved north to Chicago with his family at the age of five. His first novel, *Let Me Breathe Thunder*, was published in 1939 and his second and last, *Blood on the Forge*, was published in 1941. He spent the remainder of his career writing for radio, film, and television. He died in Los Angeles in 1986.

NICHOLAS LEMANN is the author of *The Promised Land*. He has worked at *The Washington Monthly*, *Texas Monthly*, and the *Washington Post* and since 1983 has been a national correspondent for *The Atlantic*. He lives in Westchester County, New York, with his family.